MORE THAN A
NUMBER

How the Enneagram Reveals Your Unique Lens and Essential Place in the World

NATE BEBOUT

Printed in the United States of America

First Printing, 2019

ISBN 978-1-7337624-0-3

CONTENTS

THE SURPRISING NECESSITY OF WOLVES
(Or, Why This Book Exists)

I'm going to be straight with you.

The world needs a lot of things. What it *doesn't* need, though, is another book about "self-discovery" or "becoming a better you."

Fortunately, that's not what this book is meant to be. Instead, the strategies I'll detail in this book go far beyond the realm of simplistic "self-help" advice.

Because here's the deal…

You see the world in a **unique way**. *Everyone* sees the world in their own individual, unique way.

And those individual views of the world **come into conflict every single day**.

Now that we're pushing eight billion in global population, if we're only able to see the world through our own eyes, it's no surprise there are so many conflicts.

From nation-states battling for power and resources, to toddlers scrabbling for the same action figure, conflict grows out of us like weeds in a cracked driveway.

Conflict is inevitable.

In fact, if you happen to believe your daily news feed, our world is more divided now than at any other time *in history*.

The simplistic answer to this problem is just to pluck the people we don't like out of our lives. But whether we like it or not, removing any thread from our social fabric can have some massive unintended consequences. The following story is a great example of what I mean.

Trophic Cascade

By 1920, all of the wolves in Yellowstone National Park had been hunted down or driven out of the park.

In the following seven decades, the elk and whitetail deer population exploded to the point at which, with no real predators, they were causing severe environmental damage. They had utterly destroyed river beds, trampled whatever native saplings tried to gain a footing in the area, and, in general, pushed the whole system out of whack.

Beavers, for example, all but migrated out because of a lack of adult aspens. In the past, the soil had been loosened by elk and deer hooves as they ran from predators. But without that natural aeration, native grasses now struggled to grow in the compacted soil. Coyotes, with virtually no competition for food, destroyed the habitat. The grizzlies, already endangered, died off or migrated out of the park.

In the early 1990s, however, wildlife officials began the process of reintroducing wolves back into Yellowstone in an attempt to regain some semblance of balance.

Local farmers and livestock owners put up strong opposition to this idea. They were convinced that reintroducing an apex predator to the area would threaten their livelihood—as well as their families and children.

Despite the pushback, though, in 1995 the wolves returned.

And then something magical happened.

Almost overnight the wolves began to keep the elk population in check.

Because the elk now had to stay on the move and couldn't spend their days lounging on the river banks (which had turned into stagnant marshes by this point) the streams returned to their natural flow.

Likewise, because the elk were no longer able to hang out in one place for very long, they couldn't overgraze the aspen and willow saplings. As a result, the trees came back. And with the rivers running and the trees growing, beavers returned.

What's more, because the wolves were eating the elk, the grizzly population also grew, mainly because they could steal the wolf kills.

The wolves also kept the coyote population down—which,

shockingly, reduced the number of livestock kills for the ranchers, the idea's *earliest and most vocal opposition.*

As the coyote population decreased, the red fox and rodent population returned, setting the stage for large birds like hawks and eagles to make a resurgence.

Put simply: Once the wolves came back, **the whole ecosystem started to thrive**.

Balance just... *happened.*

Why Every Thread in the Tapestry Matters

I tell this story because it's a great illustration of how we as people live together.

We need each other.

You might not be a fan of certain people—or certain kinds of people—but like it or not, they're essential. Elk certainly don't like wolves. But both are essential for the whole ecosystem to flourish.

What the world needs now is more of "you doing you."

When all of us are living out our own unique visions of the world—while at the same time understanding how everyone around us naturally approaches the world—the whole system, well... *it just works.*

Balance happens.

Peace happens.

So if "you being you" leads to balance and peace, it follows that you need to know *who* you are, and *why* you approach your life the way you do.

That's what the Enneagram offers.

It answers the two most fundamental questions we, as humans, are forever attempting to suss out:

Who am I?

And, **how do I fit into this world?**

Mirror Vs. Lens

Other self-assessment tools—like the Myers-Briggs, for example— are **mirrors**. They show you what you're *like.*

For example, here's a question from one of those assessments:

"Do you draw energy from working with groups of people?"

Let's say that's true, so you answer, "Yes."

The results: "You draw energy from working with groups of people."

All the test has done is taken off the "Do" at the beginning and replaced the question mark with a period.

That's the extent of what it can tell you.

It's a mirror.

Which is fine. That's helpful info to have, right? We have mirrors for a reason. They're important. You don't want to walk out into the world each morning without at least a quick check of what you look like at that moment.

But that mirror only shows you *what* you look like. It doesn't show you *why* you look that way... or, more importantly, **what to do with that information**.

The Enneagram, though, is a **lens**.

It shows you what the world looks like through your eyes.

It also reveals your secret motivations—those hidden parts of you that determine how you view your life.

And, in this book, you'll get some great ideas about **what to do with that information**.

_____

Nine Types, Infinite Combinations

My approach to the Enneagram is not a cookie-cutter one. Most versions of the assessment rigidly divide people into nine "Types," but I always begin with the basic (and pretty obvious) idea that there are far more than nine types of people.

I view the Enneagram as a process of self-discovery—and not as a strategy for putting people into tidy, clearly-labeled boxes.

By using the nine Enneagram Types as a starting point, you can unlock an incredible amount of information about your particular approach to—and lens on—life.

Also, my approach takes all nine of your strategies and ranks them visually. While other books on the Enneagram might give you your "number" along with a brief explanation of what that means, I've always felt that this method doesn't show you the full picture. In my experience, your lowest scores are just as important as your highest. And seeing all your scores rendered visually gives you a far more accurate view of who you really are.

You want *all* the numbers, high and low. Why? Because having that information gives you *context.* And context is necessary when it comes to understanding—not just yourself, but others as well.

A quick illustration: When it comes to choice of lenses, photographers have a ton of options. There are wide-angle, telescopic, macro, zoom, and a million other variations on a few basic themes. Some are designed specifically for low light situations. Some are perfect for action shots. Some can capture, say, a total solar eclipse without that cosmic event turning your camera into a puddle of warm goo.

But many of those lenses are expensive. Some are cumbersome to lug around. Some of them have very limited application. In short, while there are a ton of lenses available, the bulk of them just aren't terribly practical for everyday use.

That's why most professional photographers carry what's called the "nifty fifty"—a 50-millimeter lens that's great for everyday use. It's lightweight, super easy to use, focuses quickly, and works just as well for landscape shots as it does for portraits. Plus, it's relatively inexpensive compared to most other lenses of the same quality.

That's why the "nifty fifty" is the default go-to lens for photographers. In the same way, we as people each have a default lens through which we view the world. What we're looking at—what we're aiming our camera at—doesn't change. But our view of it does—based on what lens we're using.

And just like a photographer with her bag of lenses, we have access to each particular lens on the world as defined by the Enneagram's nine Types. We each have all the lenses in our bag, but we naturally settle on just one or two as our primary, natural, default lenses.

Just as every photographer's eye is different, the use of your "go-to" lens is unique. The Enneagram reveals that uniqueness—and, in the process, gives you a fantastic starting point for beginning to see **who you really are**.

This book intends to show you your primary "lens." It will also show you how much and how often you rely on the other eight lenses at your disposal.

And once you have that information? That's when things really start to get good.

Because now you can begin building strategies not just for understanding why you do what you do, but also for figuring out how you—as a single, but absolutely essential thread in our social tapestry—can best live into the role for which **you've been designed**.

HOW THE ENNEAGRAM IS SUPPOSED TO WORK

I love the old joke that, when it comes to life, everything is perfect... and then you're born, and it's all downhill from there.

For instance, consider life before you're born.

The internal human temperature is almost 100 degrees. The womb is no different. It's positively tropical in there.

Imagine that environment being the only one you've ever known, only to be launched out suddenly into a world that's freezing, blindingly bright, and where practically every corner has been honed to a sharp point.

It's the equivalent of someone pulling you out of a hot tub and tossing you into a snowdrift.

There's a whole sub-field of psychology that approaches the process of being born as the first significant trauma of our lives. A trauma, in fact, that's so severe the experience affects us on a cellular level.

So, it's no wonder that we, as humans, **develop strategies for how to both stay alive and afloat in the social currents we spend our lives navigating.**

That first strategy is crying because it's the only one we can manage.

If you've ever been around babies, their strategy becomes clear very quickly. If they're hungry, they cry. If they're sleepy, they cry. If they just want to get your attention, they cry.

Eventually, though, wailing alone doesn't cut it anymore, and they're forced to develop other strategies of varying levels of sophistication. You use certain ones every day, whether you're aware of it or not.

The brain's primary goal is to keep you alive and thriving. The Enneagram's strategies arise directly out of this goal, from the moment you're born until you die.

When determining what those strategies are, and how we implement them, there are plenty of tools available.

The Myers-Briggs, for example, is great for telling us "what" we do. Do you like spending time with people or being alone? Great! You're either an extrovert or an introvert, depending on your answer.

Likewise, the DISC Assessment (which stands for Dominance, Influence, Steadiness and Conscientiousness) is fantastic for determining "how" you approach the world around you. Is your M.O. to be task-oriented and dominant? Or are you more likely to approach life with a little more socially-focused passivity?

That's all excellent information.

But it's not the whole story. Not by a long shot.

The Importance of "Why"

Simon Sinek has risen to prominence over the past few years in the leadership consulting world. He has the ability to take complicated ideas and distill them down into digestible chunks.

In his book *Start With Why*, he draws this circle:

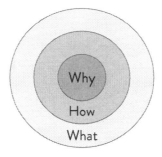

The outside ring represents the "What." At this level, we're dealing with basic information, the surface details.

What do you do? What do you make? What is your job?

Next level down is the "How." This tier essentially tells us "How" the "What" gets done. It's a slightly deeper question than "What," but not by much.

Below that, though, is the "Why." Sinek argues that **people who start with "Why" are the most compelling**.

He offers up the differences between Microsoft and Apple as an example. Both are computer companies. Both were started by visionaries. Both brands are household names. Despite the fact that most PCs are more powerful and cheaper than most of Apple's catalog, Apple's market share continues to grow each year.

Why?

Because Microsoft is excellent at telling you *what* they do. But Apple has always started at the deepest level—and offered its potential customers the *why* behind it all.

Jump onto YouTube and search "Apple think different commercial." It's one of the first television commercials they ever made. The whole video is a black and white montage of significant historical and cultural figures—Gandhi, Martin Luther King, Jr., Amelia Earhart, Jim Henson, to name just a few—with a voiceover lauding these luminaries for their radical visions of the world. The result is compelling, even inspirational. But here's the thing… nowhere does it tell you anything about what they're trying to sell you. It's all about the *why*.

People want to be a part of a grand dream. They want to get on board with a person or organization that has a big, bright vision for what can be accomplished.

And because the wisdom inscribed on the Oracle at Delphi—"Know thyself"—still holds true even now, **discovering your own "Why" is vital to becoming the happy, healthy, fully-realized social human you were designed to be.**

Answering that central question will also give you a massive amount of insight into why the people around you do what they do. More importantly, it also gives you empathy towards them.

The Enneagram reveals your motivations, your thought patterns.

It shows you why you think and behave in the ways you do.

It gives you the big, fat, monumental WHY that serves as the solution for so many of the questions at the center of what it means to be human.

The first step in figuring out those mysteries is to begin at the very beginning. And that's why the Enneagram starts with the **Centers of Intelligence**.

Centers of Intelligence

Imagine you wake up alone one day on a deserted tropical island.

For months you see no other evidence of human life. Without anyone around, you are forced into survival mode. Ambitions, goals, hopes, dreams, and the daily clutter of your past life are no longer relevant. Your concentration is on just one thing. Namely, not dying.

But then, one day, you hear a noise coming from the jungle. Fully expecting an attack, you wait at the ready.

And then…

It's a person. *Another* person.

Just like that, you're no longer alone on the island.

First, you feel shock. In the next moment, you feel a mix of fear and hope. And then, as you're caught eye-to-eye with this new stranger, the questions start piling up.

At first, you're going to wonder if this person is friend or foe. Do they mean you harm, or will they be an ally? Between the two of you, who's going to have the final say in whether you live or die?

Next, the answers to the first set of problems will lead to deeper questions about the relationship itself: What are the dynamics of this new relationship? Will they even want to engage with you? What are the costs of casting in your lot with this person? What are the benefits?

From there, you will begin to ask questions pertaining to who you are here in this new life: Who are you now? How do you preserve your identity? How does your essential self relate to the one other person on the island?

These three categories of questions serve as the basis for all the existential questions we've been asking since humanity's beginning. They also make up the **Three Centers of Intelligence**, which are **the three driving forces behind everything we do, consciously or subconsciously.**

Here's how it works...

AUTONOMY CENTER
Seeking Control

Our first concern is if we have the final say in our future. It's the first and only question at the root of all animal life—whether you're a human or not. Even amoebas are working to answer this question, albeit without the benefit of consciousness.

Within the Enneagram vernacular, these questions happen in the **Autonomy** Center with **control** as the main goal. This Center of Intelligence is also classically referred to as the "Gut Center."

AFFINITY CENTER
Seeking Belonging

In this center, the questions concern those around you and how all those disparate social pieces fit together. In our island analogy, you'll want to know the details of this new relationship.

Why? Because, once *you've* figured out how to stay alive, the next big problem is figuring out how *a whole group* of you are going to continue to survive—along with how you're going to do it together.

This second level is the **Affinity** Center, in which the highest priority is **belonging**. It's also historically been described as the "Heart Center."

IDENTITY CENTER
Seeking Safety

The third category of questions deals with who you are. What is your identity? How safe is that identity? How do you fit within your small community? What's your place within the broader global community? And finally, what's your role within the universe itself?

You want to know who you are in the grand scheme of things.

This Center is defined by **Identity** and pursues **safety**. It's traditionally referred to as the "Head Center."

BRINGING IT ALL TOGETHER

One of the main reasons I've written this book, in fact, is to reposition the starting point for how we look at the Enneagram. In the past, the emphasis has been on the head, heart, and gut… but most people are left not knowing what those distinctions actually mean.

In reality, the three Centers serve as the core for understanding why we deal with each other in the ways that we do. Ignoring this core as our starting point is like coming out of the gates at the Kentucky Derby without a horse.

You're able to move forward, sure. But you won't get very far… or very fast.

The overarching WHY of the three centers is *that important.*

Each of these centers is at work in every relationship we have.

In fact, a lack of health in any relationship happens when we give up one of them.

Codependency, for example, occurs when you give up your identity in a relationship. Animosity comes about when you give up the affinity in the relationship. Coercion or manipulation happens when you lose your autonomy in a relationship.

While it's not apparent *why* we tend to put more of our energy into one of these centers over the other two, it is clear that we *do*. For each of us, one of these centers always takes precedence.

Somewhere along the line—this is truly a blend of both nature and nurture—we subconsciously decide which one is most important. Maybe this choice happens because one of the three feels like it needs the most attention.

For example, let's say you feel like you have your life in order. Additionally, you also have close relationships with your friends and family. With those two basic needs met, your instincts may then draw your attention to all the potential threats setting off alarms in the part of your brain that's trying to keep your identity safely above water.

Or, put another way: If your Autonomy and Affinity Centers are satisfied, you'll naturally put your efforts into your Identity Center.

But, whatever the reasons for your (subconscious) choice, the fact remains that we all choose our Center. And out of that, we develop strategies for living our life.

Which brings us to the Enneagram Types.

The Nine Types

The nine Enneagram Types are divided evenly between the three Centers of Intelligence. For each Center of Intelligence, there are three overarching strategies for meeting that basic desire.

Which makes sense, right? If you lock a starving elk and a famished wolf inside a grocery store, they're both going to try to solve the same basic animal need—namely, hunger. But their strategies are going to be very different. The elk is going to head for the produce section and the wolf, if he's smart and avoids trying to wrestle down the elk all by his lonesome, is going to make a dash for the frozen meats.

To put it into human terms, think about it like this…

Despite the fact that both you and I want, say, *affinity* above all else, we could very well approach that goal from opposite angles. Just because you and I might ultimately want the same thing, the lenses we see through—along with the strategies we use—might be wildly different.

As with the Centers of Intelligence, no one is going to be exclusively one Type. You are more than just a number. Instead, as with everything in the assessment, it's always going to be a question of *emphasis*.

One of the remarkable things about the Enneagram, in fact, is that it factors in the basic truth that humans are messy, inconsistent creatures. It also shows which other Types we're most likely to draw strategies from—both in good times and bad.

And beyond just figuring out which distinct Type you are, the assessment results focus on both your highest and lowest scores. Although *Parks and Recreation*'s Ron Swanson would have us believe that "crying is only acceptable at funerals and the Grand Canyon," our weaknesses are just as critical as our strengths.

Knowing *why* you or others happen to perform poorly in certain situations is just as important as knowing why you find success in others.

These strengths and weaknesses are plotted out over what I call the **Type Matrix**.

To illustrate why this approach is essential to our understanding of people beyond just labeling them as a "number," check out this Type Matrix. Mine is blue, and my wife's is red.

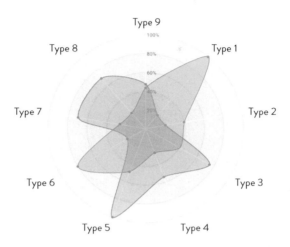

Not a lot of overlap, huh?

I should add that with any other Enneagram assessment, these results would be far less detailed.

(To take your Enneagram assessment, go to test.natebebout.com.)

For instance, if I had just said, "I'm a Type Five, and my wife is a Type One," that doesn't even begin to give you a full picture of our strengths and weaknesses. In fact, it doesn't tell you much of anything about how our particular strategies complement each other.

But with the Type Matrix, you can see far more nuance in the relationship. You can get a decent idea of who we are as people. You can also see *how we fit together*.

For example, take a look at her score in Type Six (which is defined primarily by loyalty to the group). Her score is pretty high, right? Well, now take a look at my score in the same category. Apparently, given the sub-basement depth of my Type Six score, I might not be the one you want to count on to go down with the ship.

You can also see that I score pretty high in the domination-oriented Type Eight, while her score there lands somewhere close to zero on the Kelvin scale.

These insights are valuable.

Merely saying "I'm a Type Five and my wife is a Type One" is the equivalent of claiming to be a great philanthropist after dropping off a load of gently used polo shirts at Goodwill. It's technically correct, I guess, but there's *a lot* of unexplored nuance there.

So, knowing the details is important. The good news for our marriage is that we work well together because of these corresponding strengths and weaknesses.

This Type Matrix pattern within relationships tends to happen quite a bit. As if to reinforce the idea that we all need each other, our natural tendency is to seek out partners and spouses that (to quote reluctantly from *Jerry Maguire*) "complete us."

Understanding your underlying motivations—along with those of others around you—will unlock the mysteries that exist below the surface of all your social interactions.

This clarity is the first step toward bringing balance—and empathy—to the system.

And, speaking of balance, keep the following in mind whenever you're considering the Enneagram Types:

The etymological root of the English word "gift" is translated in other languages as the word "poison." What allows you to build your empire can also be the same thing that enslaves others—or even what brings your own civilization to ruin.

The same thing that makes you great at what you do can also be your undoing in other parts of your life.

This idea of the double-edged sword will be a theme for each of the nine Enneagram Types.

Once again, it's all about balance. That and using your God-given superpowers for good and not evil.

HOW TO USE THIS BOOK

STEP 1
Take the Assessment

First, go to **natebebout.com** and take the assessment. You can certainly read this book without taking the test, but being able to reference your results as we go through each of the nine Types will be a far more enlightening experience.

If you're familiar with the Enneagram, you might be tempted to skip to your previously defined Type. But, as I said before, we're not just one Type. Just knowing that you are, say, a Type Six is a fantastic starting point. But you've only scratched the first layer of soil.

There's a lot more to discover beneath all those layers.

And speaking of layers...

STEP 2
Read On!

For the sake of clarity, here's how I've organized this book.

After taking a look at each Type from a 1,000-foot view, we'll do a hard zoom down to the core of what makes you tick. From there, we'll move, layer by layer, out from the most hidden desire—that fiery ball of essential motivation in the center that no one really sees—to the surface-level details that the rest of the world sees when they look at you.

How Each Type Description Works

These different layers aren't just random, disconnected attributes of each Type. They're foundational blocks that build upon one another, starting with our deepest longings—revealed through the Center of Intelligence—and moving out to the most external expressions of our personality–such as the Speaking Style. Each of us compiles our worldview in layers, starting with our core. Consider the following sections as the different layers of geological strata that make up Planet You. Here's the structure:

CENTER OF INTELLIGENCE

As I mentioned before, the Center of Intelligence is where you need to start when you're doing a deep dive into who you—and those you interact with each day—really ARE. Everything about you builds upon this core.

PRIMARY STRATEGY

Here we'll go far beyond simple "Types" and instead explore the basic strategies you and others naturally rely on in everyday life. Based on the underlying Center of Intelligence, in this section we'll go deep into what makes up your "default" strategies for living in this universe.

SELF-IMAGE

We are all used to dressing the part for certain activities and events. You may wear a business suit to work or a jersey to support your favorite sports team, but underneath all of those outfits and costumes is your self-image. Forget what others are seeing. Self-image is how you view yourself in your own mind.

WHO'S ON YOUR SHOULDER?

You remember the old *Looney Tunes* cartoons where any moral choice for a character is depicted by an angel on one shoulder and a devil on the other? It's the same thing here.

Your self-image also comes with a voiceover. This inner voice continually runs through your head. Informed by both your Center of Intelligence and your primary strategy, this voice continually reinforces the "why" behind the "what" and "how" of your daily life.

AVOIDANCE

Consider this section a detailed chemical breakdown of your own personal Kryptonite. In understanding why you're heading in a particular direction—and not another—it's vital to understand what you're attempting to avoid.

FIGHTING WORDS

We all have cracks in our armor. In this section we'll explore which weaponized words not only get through those seams... but also do the most damage.

DEFENSE MECHANISM

Defense mechanisms are reflexive responses when a person feels unsafe. Just as you might duck or put up your hands if someone threw a ball at you suddenly, humans have psychological reflexes that protect us from thoughts and ideas we do not like.

MANIPULATION

This section explores how we impose our own worldview on others. Our manipulation strategies are how we attempt to force others to see us the way we see ourselves.

SPEAKING STYLE

Whenever we open our mouths, we reveal a lot about who we are. Each Type tends to have a particular way of speaking. Understanding these idiosyncrasies in how we communicate goes a long way in building empathy—both for ourselves and others.

WINGS (W)

No one is purely just one Enneagram Type. Instead, everyone is a unique mixture of their basic, "default" Type and one of the two Types situated next to it on the outer perimeter of the Enneagram. The two Types adjacent to your primary Type are your wings.

COMPLEMENTARY STRATEGIES

In the same way that most of us pull from a particular strategy adjacent to our primary Type, so too do we pull from two other Types. What those strategies look like often depends on how well we're doing mentally, physically, and spiritually. When we're doing well, we take that action in "security." When we're not doing so hot, we make that move under "stress."

(In other Enneagram books, you'll see these described as points of "integration" and "disintegration." The reason I call these "complementary strategies" is because they are natural secondary and tertiary strategies to your primary strategy.)

Also, within this section, we'll take a look at how these

complementary strategies work on a practical level.

When it comes to other people, there are three basic ways you can interact with them. You can move **toward** them, **away from** them, or **against** them. Each Type borrows strategies from its complementary Type depending on how that person is engaging with others.

For example: Type Ones draw their complementary strategies from Types Four and Seven. Type Ones move **against** others by criticizing, Type Sevens move **towards** others for enjoyment, and Type Fours move **away from** others for attention. So, when a Type One is feeling happy and social, they may borrow from the Seven and engage with others in a positive way.

Knowing how these strategies interact in everyday situations is vital for truly understanding both yourself and others.

So, there it is.

Take the test, turn the page, and let's dig in!

TYPE ONE
The Good Person

_____

When my wife Leah was in high school, she was assigned a particularly challenging paper.

She read what she was supposed to, allotted plenty of time to get it all done, and sat down to write it.

It went pretty well at first. She plugged away for at least a good four, maybe five minutes.

And then it happened.

My father-in-law recalls her crashing into the living room, throwing herself face-down on the couch, and sobbing in turmoil. She spent the rest of the evening in complete angst over the project. Why? Because, she knew all the things she *could* write about. But, she didn't know what the teacher *expected*.

She wasn't clear on what the rules were.

My wife scores very high within the Type One category. So, that meant (and still means) a lot of self-imposed pressure, a lot of worries about following the rules, a lot of doing things right as well as being perceived to have done them right.

It meant that, yes, she agonized over the assignment. But it also meant that when grades came back, hers was (of course) a solid A+.

The Good Person

Type Ones are amazing.

They tend to be idealistic perfectionists, fastidious, legalistic, meticulous, and highly conscientious. While others might lob the descriptor "anal-retentive" in their direction, their attention to detail is an incredible asset for any community fortunate enough to have them as a member. They also tend toward righteousness (in legal, moral, and even spiritual contexts) and work very hard to remain blameless in the eyes of others.

Type Ones throughout history have been some of our most exceptional teachers, our most powerful forces for social and political change. Type Ones are devoted to making things better, not only for themselves, but also for others.

On the positive side of things, their standards are very high. On the negative end of the equation, their standards are very high.

Meaning: Their drive towards perfectionism can both propel them to heroic levels of accomplishment, especially within the social justice sphere, and at the same time make them critical, resentful and,

well, pretty super judgey. Though they can seem high-strung and unrelenting in their expectations, Ones are earnest and consistent.

CENTER OF INTELLIGENCE
The Core Psychological Need of Type Ones

Remember, the first thing to pay attention to with each of these nine Types are the underlying Centers of Intelligence.

In the case of Ones—along with their counterparts, the Eights and Nines—the goal is **Autonomy. Above all else, these three Types want to make sure that their fates are in their own hands.** This third of the Enneagram is populated with the control freaks (although not always in the typical ways you might expect, which I'll get to in later chapters).

Their "Why" is to make sure they never get trapped in a situation they won't be able to escape. They don't want to be beholden to anyone, to "owe" anyone anything they might not be able to deliver on. They tend to have high levels of instinctual survival skills. They have a "gut level" style of knowing. And because they're hell-bent on remaining indomitable, anger can often serve as a powerful motivator.

PRIMARY STRATEGY
How Ones Protect Themselves from the Unknown

Type Ones defend themselves by **following the rules.**

Back in college, I remember driving home from a concert with a group of friends. It was late, three or four in the morning. My town is a lot of things—most of them great—but one thing that it's not is a bustling metropolis. So, as we drove down through the center of town back to the university, there were no other cars on the road.

We pulled up to a red light and waited.

And waited.

And then waited some more.

When it became apparent that the light was not going to turn green anytime before the next ice age, I shrugged and announced that I was *just going to go.* After all, traffic lights are important. But only in the spirit of the law. Plus, we were all exhausted.

I didn't get pushback from any of my fellow weary travelers… except for one. A buddy who just so happens to score very high in Type One.

"You can't run a red light," he said, visibly shaken by this apparent anarchic streak he hadn't noticed in my character until just this moment.

"There are no other cars around," I said. "Literally. There are exactly zero cars."

"I know," my buddy said, his eyes wide with something akin to existential terror. "But you can't just run a red light. It's *against the law.*"

This illustration gives you a ton of insight into the strategies Type Ones use. His reaction to breaking a rule—even when common sense would dictate that breaking the rule is beneficial for everyone involved—shows precisely how exacting Type Ones are when it comes to their need to remain above reproach. They simply can't give anyone—including themselves—a single reason to question their ethical probity.

Unassailability, for the Type One, is paramount. Blamelessness is vital. Without integrity, all is lost. The letter of the law is unbendable.

So much so, in fact, that I'm convinced that if my buddy had been driving, ten years later we'd still be sitting at that stupid light.

SELF-IMAGE
How Ones View Themselves in Light of Their Strategy

"I am righteous."

These are the three words that allow Type Ones to function, from dawn until dusk, and all the fraught hours in between.

Their ability to control what goes on around them—to make sure that they are simultaneously not taking advantage of others or being taken advantage of by them—depends almost entirely on the idea that they are blameless.

And if you're coming in for any sort of moral audit? Bring your abacus. They've kept all their receipts.

For Ones, these three words are paramount for their dealings with the world—not just externally, but also internally.

It's all well and good for a Type One if the world views them as unassailable, blameless, and without reproach. But what these traits reveal is that the external view—no matter how rosy—just isn't enough. The Type One also has to maintain an internal sense of consistency as well.

Type Ones need to *know* that they're blameless in their own eyes.

WHO'S ON YOUR SHOULDER?
The Voice on Repeat Inside a One's Head

For the Type One, the entity perched on their collarbone is an annoying **proofreader** who can pick out any and every misplaced comma. The direction from that entity is both clear and repetitive: Follow the rules and remain blameless. Your control over life is entirely dependent upon it.

Type Ones are extremely sensitive to any and all criticism... even if that criticism isn't directed at them.

Having forsaken their "wants" for "oughts," Ones can hear that inner voice admonishing them for not being *perfect enough.*

AVOIDANCE
The Thing Ones Must Avoid According to Their Strategy

What does a Type One avoid at all costs?

Being morally wrong. In any way.

Why? Because "being morally wrong," in the mind of the Type One, equates one-to-one with "losing your control over the situation."

And again—the horse is dead, I know, but it bears re-beating—that motivation flows directly from the underlying Center of Intelligence: that perpetual quest for **Autonomy**.

Consequently, if control equates to self-imposed order, any crack in that dam threatens every village downstream. This leads to the Type One's hypersensitivity to correction. Every simple, normal, human mistake they make feels like a colossal failure.

FIGHTING WORDS
The Weaponized Language Most Likely to Find Its Way
Through the Seams in a One's Armor

"You are an immoral, unprincipled deadbeat."

Want to demoralize a Type One? Attack their integrity. Question their motivations. Shine a light on any chink in that armor of unassailability.

DEFENSE MECHANISM
How Ones Reaffirm Their Paradigm to Themselves

Ones reinforce their self-image through a process called **reaction formation.** Reaction formation is a fancy German psychological term for the following idea:

You want to knock off work and play video games. But you know that doing so isn't right. So you keep working and later, instead of playing video games, you start a blog about how video games are ruining our culture.

The reaction formation process happens when you desire something that you know is wrong and, in a display of classic overcompensation, turn the rejection of that thing up, in true Spinal Tap style, from one to eleven.

Given their innate drive for ethical consistency, Type Ones will often take up arms against the things that they desperately want but simultaneously find morally repugnant. This helps maintain their self-image as a righteous person. A One consistently does what is *needed* or what they *ought* to do, rather than giving in to what they actually desire.

MANIPULATION
How Ones Impose Their Paradigm on Others

Ones make sure everyone around them knows that they are rule-following, upright citizens by **criticizing or correcting others**.

Here's how manipulation strategies work: They take the voice from "Who's on Your Shoulder" above and direct it outward. So, just as the Type One feels that constant pressure from their inner voice to follow the rules and maintain perfection, the way they attempt to get others to take the same approach is to redirect the megaphone out towards the world at large.

Type Ones don't expect you to live up to their own internal demands. But they do want to remind you that they are right.

Type Ones take the moral imperative that drives them and aim it out into the world, towards others.

SPEAKING STYLE
How Ones Communicate with Others

The genre of a One's speech can be broadly defined as **preaching**.

If you are fortunate to have a Type One in your life and you do something in their presence that they fundamentally disagree with, you're going to hear, in exquisite detail, an apologetic presentation that would put the late Billy Graham to shame.

They want to convince you that the way they are doing something is the only way anyone should ever do it.

Most of the time, this advice comes from the goodness of their ridiculously good hearts. What can sometimes feel like nagging is often just a One's effort to make everyone's life easier.

WINGS (W)
The Strategies on Either Side of Type One

The Type One's wings are **Nine and Two**.

1W9 - The Idealist
Here, the perfectionism of the Type One meets the wishfulness of the Type Nine. The 1W9 wants to see the whole world set right—world peace brought about through economic and political justice. They're principled and purposeful, but can also fall into the trap of becoming too judgmental. They're a little more high-strung than their 1W2 counterparts.

1W2 - The Advocate
The 1W2 combines the righteousness of the Type One with the helpfulness of the Type Two. They tend to be caring in their service and leadership, demanding in their insistence on making a difference, and hell-bent on reform, in whatever context that might occur.

COMPLEMENTARY STRATEGIES
The Two Strategies that Round Out Type One

Type One's complementary strategies draw from Types **Four and Seven**.

Type Ones move *against* others by criticizing.
Type Sevens move *towards* others for enjoyment.
Type Fours move *away* from others for attention.

At their best, Type Ones pull from the high ends of these two Types.

When they aren't particularly healthy, they pull from the low sides.

In moments of security, Ones move toward the strategies of a Seven. This shift can look wildly different depending on their level of health.

A healthy One will move to the high side of Seven where their exacting nature softens a bit and they relax. They tend to begin asking the question, "What do I *want* to do?" as opposed to their default query, "What am I *supposed* to do?"

On the low side of Seven, however, Ones become self-indulgent and escapist, choosing to do what they want without any regard for the consequences. This is the idealistic, justice-seeking TV lawyer who, after losing a case during which she did everything right, slips into disillusionment and goes out on a bender. Great for the drama, not so good for the character herself.

Under stress, Ones move to Type Four.

When healthy Ones shift to the high side of Four, they'll take a break from that constant drive toward obligation and stop to consider what sort of self-care they need.

On the low side of Type Four, however, Ones that haven't achieved their goals get melodramatic and overwhelmed. They may also start to view themselves as martyrs.

Why We All Need the Ones

Type Ones are on a mission. They want to make things better. Across the globe and throughout time, the course of history would be wildly different without Ones stepping out of their daily routine and working to solve what they see as injustice.

Sir Thomas More, for example, opted for prison and abuse at the hands of the King of England instead of turning his back on his faith. His courage has since inspired countless others to hold fast to their beliefs, undeterred by whatever persecution they might be facing.

Jimmy Carter could've easily left the United States presidency, sat back on his laurels, and spent the rest of his life cashing speaking-fee checks. He might not have been the most effective leader of the free world, but because of his dedication to advancing quality-of-life efforts on a global scale, no one can challenge his status as a giant among humanitarians in the decades since.

Most people don't know that Mahatma Gandhi left a growing family and a promising law career to become an activist for Indian independence. After experiencing the racism and maltreatment of his people at the hands of the British Empire, his commitment to nonviolent civil disobedience set the tone for future activists in their peaceful resistance against tyranny.

And those are just a few examples. Type Ones are wonderful and necessary, both on a global and personal level. They often serve as the moral compass for the community. They also have the guts to stand up for what they believe, even when the odds are clearly stacked against them. They are unstoppable forces for change, defeating evil and planting the flag for righteousness… and then serving as a stabilizing force once the new order has been established.

After all, the One is referred to as "The Good Person." And you certainly can't have too many of those in this chaotic, broken world.

OVERVIEW

Type One: The Good Person

Center of Intelligence AUTONOMY

Primary Strategy FOLLOWING THE RULES

Self Image "I AM RIGHTEOUS."

Who's on Your Shoulder THE PROOFREADER

Avoidance BEING MORALLY WRONG

Fighting Words "YOU ARE AN IMMORAL DEADBEAT."

Defense Mechanism REACTION FORMATION

Manipulation CRITICISM & CORRECTION

Speaking Style PREACHING

Wings TYPES 9 & 2

Complementary Strategies TYPES 4 & 7

②
TYPE TWO
The Loving Person

―――――――――

There's an episode of *I Dream of Jeannie* that begins with a knock on the front door. Jeannie, blinking out of her Persian garb into a modern green house dress, greets a visitor and invites him in. The man asks if Major Nelson is around. Jeannie replies that he's getting ready for work and while the visitor waits for the Major, he wanders around the living room, criticizing the blandness of the decor.

Jeannie, wishing only to help the Major, takes umbrage at the snide remarks and begins to manifest various priceless treasures around the room that are meant to impress the man—who at one point refers to the house's overall style as "Grand Rapids Renaissance." What starts with a Louis XV marquetry commode, an original Renoir, and a Ming vase, ends with a safe full of cash and an entire cast of chefs and servants attending to the house.

When Major Nelson emerges from his room, adjusting his cufflinks and straightening his tie, the visitor finally introduces himself.

"Hello, Major," he says. "My name is Harry Huggins… from the

Internal Revenue Service."

If you've ever seen *I Dream of Jeannie*, you know that every episode follows essentially these same beats. Jeannie wants to help Major Nelson. But because she doesn't understand the nuances of modern life, she ends up causing more trouble for him.

His problems arise because whenever she perceives his needs, she prioritizes them above everything else. The whole series is a case study in an out-of-balance Type Two.

The Loving Person

Type Twos are nurturing, outwardly-focused, and very sociable. They will give you the shirt off their back or help you move a 500-pound armoire with only five minutes' notice. They tend to be warm and giving.

If you're ever in a situation where you've been beaten, robbed, and left for dead on the road to Samaria, pray there's a Two coming along in the very near future.

Type Twos are well-intentioned and at their best are selfless, encouraging, and supportive. They are everyone's assistant. While others seek the spotlight, Twos would rather serve in an unobtrusive way in order to support the team.

Type Twos also tend to have problems with self-care. They can easily slip into the trap of defining their whole identity by how much they are needed by others. Even *recognizing* their own needs can be difficult.

CENTER OF INTELLIGENCE
The Core Psychological Need of Type Twos

With Type Two, we've now shifted into the **Affinity** Center of Intelligence (which also includes Types Three and Four).

The hallmark of this section of the Enneagram is emotional intelligence. **The main goal for Affinity Types is belonging.** They want to be accepted by others.

Although Twos, Threes, and Fours all go about this in remarkably different ways, that underlying drive is still the same.

Affinity centers are fantastic at reading others. They are social animals. They are "people-people"—although I will warn you that this doesn't always manifest in ways you might expect.

Type Twos in particular tend to be emotionally honest and open. Shame can be a substantial negative motivator. (This negative motivator applies to Threes and Fours, as well.)

PRIMARY STRATEGY
How Twos Protect Themselves from the Unknown

Twos ensure their necessity by **helping others**.

Belonging, for the Two, is the ultimate goal. Type Twos want to be indispensable. They go about this by making sure that the needs of others are met. Their focus is eternally outward.

When they hear the word "need," they feel the word "obligation."

As non-Twos, we have to be careful not to take advantage of

members of this Type. If you're tired and merely muse out loud that you could "really use a cup of coffee," the Type Two is going to interpret those words as if they were meant specifically for them.

A friend of mine owns a marketing business in town, and one of the employees is a Two. Because of this knowledge, his team will often joke with the Two that they "really needed some milkshakes." This particularly delightful Two obviously knows they're kidding. But just like clockwork, she'll still return after her lunch break with all the ingredients to make everyone a milkshake.

A Two cannot, try as they might, walk past any need—no matter how small—without trying to meet it.

 SELF-IMAGE
How Twos View Themselves in Light of Their Strategy

"I am helpful."

Type Twos don't need help. They are the helpers… whether you need it or not (as in the case of every episode of *I Dream of Jeannie*.)

Part of this self-image is the idea that "I am the only person around here who really has their stuff together."

Their basic mode of operation is to consider their own needs already met so they can then help everyone around them. And often, whatever need they might have is projected out onto others.

If you go on vacation with a Type Two, they'll be packed up and loaded up before you've even decided which toothbrush to take. They'll aid you with that decision and then help you pack your underwear too.

WHO'S ON YOUR SHOULDER?
The Voice on Repeat Inside a Two's Head

The inner-dialogue of a Two is that of the **ultimate concierge,** complete with a constant hissing tape loop of "I could've done more."

The voice from the Type Two's shoulder is constantly scanning the room... Who needs their drink refilled? Who needs their pillow fluffed? Who could use a few gentle swipes of a lint roller?

They are always telling themselves that "I'm on top of it. I'm fine. It's everyone else who needs my help."

Type Twos ultimately want to belong, but it's not entirely altruistic. The expectation is that if they help others, those same others won't reject them. If they take care of others, they'll ultimately be taken care of by others.

Twos have a tendency to expect those around them to be mind-readers, adopting their own beloved Type Two tactics of helpfulness.

This expectation is why, if they don't feel the care they've been offering is being reciprocated, Twos can have a Hindenburg-esque explosion that brings down everything around them.

AVOIDANCE
The Thing Twos Must Avoid According to Their Strategy

Type Twos tend to avoid **their own needs**. Why? Because if they don't, they feel like they'll become irrelevant, unloved, and left out in the cold.

They want to be indispensable, but they want to accomplish that goal from behind the scenes.

My administrative assistant is a Type Two. She will not go on vacation unless I make her. And even then, it takes some convincing.

Type Twos are so focused on the needs of others that the self can easily become not just an afterthought, but *not a thought at all.*

FIGHTING WORDS
The Weaponized Language Most Likely to Find Its Way Through the Seams in a Two's Armor

"Wow, you sure are needy today!"

Want to wreck a Type Two's week? Just offer the slightest hint that they're too self-centered, and they'll spiral out like a dying quasar.

DEFENSE MECHANISM
How Twos Reaffirm Their Paradigm to Themselves

In order to bolster the belief that they should be constantly focusing on others, Twos end up engaging in classic **repression**.

Type Twos often end up in nursing or caretaker roles, which are incredibly demanding careers. The way they deal with the stress— the way they reaffirm the paradigm through which they view themselves—is to take it all, ball it up, and shove it down as deep as possible.

"Too bad," they say. "Such is life. Suck it up and get back to helping."

Though they're sweet as pie, under the surface Twos struggle with pride. "I'm not the kind of person who needs help," they will say to themselves even in situations where help is very much needed.

MANIPULATION
How Twos Impose Their Paradigm on Others

So, how does a Type Two get others on board with the idea that, as a Two, they're the indispensable helper?

They foster **codependency**.

"Codependency" is a fancy psychology term that simply means you become a bit of a barnacle on everyone else's hull. Routine things that human beings do by themselves—shopping for socks, washing your windows, even just filling up the car at the gas station— become joint ventures when organized by the Two.

If your shoelaces are untied, a Two might say, "Don't bother bending over. I'm already down here scrubbing the floor. I got it!"

SPEAKING STYLE
How Twos Communicate with Others

Always wanting to lend a hand, Twos speak through **advice-giving**.

A lot (if not most) sentences uttered by a Type Two will begin with the following phrases.

"Here's how I can help…"

"Do you need help with…?"

"Have you tried…?"

"Here's what you should do…"

If this sounds like someone in your life, you're more than likely dealing with a Two.

WINGS (W)
The Strategies on Either Side of Type Two

The Two's "wings" are **One and Three**.

2W1 - The Servant
In this wing, the empathy of the Two meets the morality of the One. The Servant is eternally driven to love others and guide them toward health.

They are warm, serving, people-pleasing, and really, really want you to feel better.

2W3 - The Host
Here, support meets giftedness. The Host is focused on setting the stage for others to succeed. They are friendly, encouraging, adaptable to the needs of others, and can often be status-seeking along the way.

COMPLEMENTARY STRATEGIES
The Two Strategies that Round Out Type Two

Type Two's complementary strategies are sourced from Types **Eight and Four**.

Type Twos move *toward* others by serving.
Type Eights move *against* others by imposing.
Type Fours move *away* from others for attention.

At their healthiest, the Type Two will pull from the high, healthy ends of these two Types. When things aren't going well, they pull from the low sides of these complementaries.

In security, Twos lean toward the strategies of Type Four.

When a healthy Two pulls from the high side of Type Four, instead of focusing all their energy on the needs of others, they'll spend some of those resources on taking care of themselves.

The unhealthy shift to Four happens when the Two feels a lack of reciprocity from others. In response, they will grow frustrated and entitled and feel no small amount of martyrdom.

When stressed, Twos make a beeline for Type Eight strategies.

A healthy Two pulls from the high side of Eight. Instead of ignoring their own needs, the Two will set boundaries, do a little self-care, and say "no."

The unhealthy shift to Eight happens when that sense of belonging they're constantly looking for disappears. They can then become aggressive, curt, hyper-independent, and manipulative.

Every mother-in-law on every sitcom ever serves as a good example for what this shift looks like.

Why We All Need the Twos

Type Twos are amazing to have in your life. Without them, communities would very quickly devolve into a self-centered, heartless, overly-ambitious, overly-narcissistic, and totally isolated collection of monsters. Plus, very little would get done. Your socks would be eternally unwashed. I promise you.

(Author's note: Obviously, I'm joking. Even the most ardent narcissists do their own laundry from time to time. But, you get the point.)

Because Twos need to be loved—and reveal that need by being very loving toward others—they provide a lot of the heart necessary for a healthy community to thrive.

The other side of the coin, however, is that the rest of us need to be very careful not to take advantage of these loving members in our circle. I'm not snatching any of their personal agency away from them—Twos are strong in ways the rest of us can't imagine—but of all the Types, the Twos are probably the most easily manipulated. Again, they will make you milkshakes for days if you let it happen.

(For the record, I am fundamentally opposed to attempting to manipulate people once you know their main Enneagram strategy. So, be nice.)

Throughout history, Twos have made an incredible impact on the lives around them.

Bishop Desmond Tutu, for example, was a South African Anglican cleric who served as both Bishop of Johannesburg and Archbishop of Cape Town in the 1980s—the first black man to hold either position. He was a vocal critic of apartheid and fought for its end. He has spent most of his life working to give a voice to the oppressed around the world, for which he received a Nobel Peace Prize.

Another Two who made a big impact on history was Eleanor Roosevelt. After losing both parents early in life, she became extraordinarily nurturing to those around her. In fact, even after discovering that her husband Franklin Roosevelt was having an affair with her own secretary, she agreed to remain in the marriage—not as a wife, but instead as a partner. And while she continued to take care of her husband as his health declined, she also took her loving nature and applied it to humanitarian causes across the globe.

Although his historical impact probably won't reach the levels of my previous two examples, fitness instructor and actor Richard Simmons is also a great example of a Two—both in his highs and his lows. When healthy, his story is one of someone who needs to be needed—and will consequently do anything to help others. His positive impact on others' lives has been well-documented. During his low points, though, when it's clear that he feels like that outpouring of love is going unrequited, he disengages and becomes a martyr. You can sense his bitterness in the interviews he gives during these low points.

If you're not a Two, you certainly have at least one in your life. And because of that, be sure to show your appreciation for them today. While other Types are responsible for making the world spin, Type Twos' hearts go a long way in keeping the whole planet in orbit.

OVERVIEW
Type Two: The Loving Person

Center of Intelligence AFFINITY

Primary Strategy HELPING OTHERS

Self Image "I AM HELPFUL."

Who's on Your Shoulder THE ULTIMATE CONCIERGE

Avoidance THEIR OWN NEEDS

Fighting Words "WOW, YOU SURE ARE NEEDY."

Defense Mechanism REPRESSION

Manipulation CODEPENDENCY

Speaking Style ADVICE GIVING

Wings TYPES 1 & 3

Complementary Strategies TYPES 8 & 4

❸
TYPE THREE
The Effective Person

Consider John. He's the CEO of a regional insurance company. His wife and two children are beautiful and perpetually put together. He serves on the school board, drives a mid-sized foreign luxury sport coupe, and handles as many business meetings as he can on the back nine of the local country club.

John is successful… and looks the part. He's direct, gets what he wants, and seems sincere even when he's not. Plus, his grill has an onboard smoker, while you're still using one of those circular charcoal-burning ones. He's winning, no matter what the situation. And he makes darn sure you know it.

Here's the thing: I just made John up.

But you know him.

Why?

Because everyone knows a Type Three.

They are fast-paced, strong-willed, make great leaders, and always seem to have their stuff together.

They love coming up with strategies and implementing them. Type Threes are drawn to leadership roles and, thanks to their competitive nature, generally get there years earlier than everyone else expected.

The goal is always to win. But it doesn't stop there.

As they're trying to beat you, they do it with aplomb. For Type Threes, style points count for double.

The Threes were probably the first people in history to employ the *fake it till you make it* strategy.

The Effective Person

Type Threes are success-oriented. They want to win. They're exceptionally adaptive, confident, and know what they're doing (no matter what that thing happens to be).

They want to succeed.

No, scratch that.

They want to *exceed*.

Type Threes tend to be highly conscious of the image they're projecting. They're very social animals and often find their way into careers with a high degree of attendant status. There are classic Type Three careers: airline pilots, astronauts, entrepreneurs, CEOs, and any number of other high-powered, high-visibility jobs that little kids tend to list out when you ask about their future goals and dreams.

Put simply: Type Threes get stuff done.

A Three will beat you to your destination and declare himself the winner, despite the fact that you weren't aware it was even a race.

CENTER OF INTELLIGENCE
The Core Psychological Need of Type Threes

With the Type Three, we're still in the **Affinity** pie slice.

Type Twos try to make themselves indispensable by helping. Type Fours hope to achieve the same goal by setting themselves apart as unique and necessary—which I'll explain in the next chapter.

The Threes want the same thing—to belong, to be necessary. In order to make that happen, their strategy is to accomplish so much that the people around them can't help but need them.

They want to belong, but their strategy is an interesting one. While other Types might try to gain your affection by allowing you to, say, beat them at tennis, Threes flip that strategy on its head.

Forget sympathy. Forget compromise. Forget propping up others. Type Threes will try to beat you at everything, utterly and completely… **and want you to love them for it**.

They want to demolish you in the primaries and then charm you into endorsing them for the general election.

And you know what? More often than not, we do.

PRIMARY STRATEGY
How Threes Protect Themselves from the Unknown

Type Threes want to **win at any cost**.

Type Threes also want to impress you. Their drive toward victory is how they make order out of the chaos.

Type Threes are often referred to as chameleons. They direct a significant amount of their energy toward appearing successful no matter the context. The chameleon descriptor is apt because success looks different depending on the situation.

For example, every politician has footage taken of him touring a factory. How do they dress in those situations? In every instance, they have on a hardhat and Carhartts. Why? Because that's what success looks like in that situation. Find them at a black-tie event, and they'll be dressed to the nines.

Funny but true: Type Threes have an outfit for everything. When they go golfing, they'll dress like a golfer. Whereas sweats and a ratty v-neck T-shirt might be your go-to for a relaxing night at home, the Three will have a nice "lounging outfit" at hand.

SELF-IMAGE
How Threes View Themselves in Light of Their Strategy

"I am successful."

Type Threes fear being a "nobody." They want to be successful. It's interesting, though... their definition of what that means is often determined by their community. For upper-class elites, for example, that might be working on Wall Street or becoming a politician.

Within a religious community, that might be becoming a pastor.
I imagine that if you were raised in an isolated garbage dump, the
Three would spend all day attempting to build the biggest tire fire in
history.

It's about context. It's also about that internal dialogue that
consistently pushes the Three to achieve more and more.

WHO'S ON YOUR SHOULDER?
The Voice on Repeat Inside a Three's Head

Because they are amazingly adept at reading a room and delivering
the right lines, the inner dialogue of a Three is that of a **political
advisor**.

Before anything comes out of their mouths, Type Threes run it
through a filter. They check for accuracy, tone, how it's going to
play in the room, and a hundred other things that could potentially
influence how successful those words are going to make them sound.

But the win-at-all-costs strategy doesn't stop with what they say. I
know Threes who won't do things if they know they're not going to
succeed. If they can't win the game, there's a decent chance they won't
even play.

AVOIDANCE
The Thing Threes Must Avoid According to Their Strategy

Type Threes are constantly battling against **failure**, in all its forms.

I have a good friend who owns a local business and is a Three. A few
years ago, I was working through the Enneagram with his employees.
As a part of my consultation, we did an activity in which each person

attempted to "make friends" with the thing they typically avoid.

A Type Two, for example, might be able to find something good about turning their focus away from everyone else's needs to do a little self-care from time to time. Or, Ones might see the benefit of not being so critical of themselves for a few minutes each day.

But when I asked my friend the Three about how failure might be a good thing, he couldn't come up with anything.

"You don't think that not winning once in awhile might be beneficial?" I asked.

"No."

"Like, nothing? It wouldn't be a learning opportunity, maybe? Or a chance to gain a new perspective on things?"

He thought for a moment.

"Anything?" I asked.

"Nope," he said finally. "I've got nothing."

That's about as Three as Three can be.

 FIGHTING WORDS
The Weaponized Language Most Likely to Find Its Way
Through the Seams in a Three's Armor

"You are a non-contributing loser."

Holy cow. If you're aching to be forced to endure a best of seven arm-wrestling match, just challenge a Three's sense of achievement. Add in a dig about how little a Three has contributed socially, and you've just started a nuclear war.

With a Three, for good or bad, it's always about escalation.

DEFENSE MECHANISM
How Threes Reaffirm Their Paradigm to Themselves

Type Threes deal with the chaos of the world by reaffirming their strategy to themselves through a process called **identification.**

This term means that Threes often **confuse their "self" with the role they play**.

With Threes, the danger is that in their pursuit of success at all costs, one of those costs can be their own identity. When so much of your focus is on what others think about you, it's easy to sacrifice your core self at the altar of success.

Currently, one of the most at-risk demographics for suicides are white, retired CEOs. Why? Because now that they're no longer running a large business—acquiring assets, implementing financial strategies, kicking corporate butt, etc.—they lose sight of who they are. They no longer know what they want. They don't know how to kick back and relax. They've spent their lives viewing themselves as a CEO instead of a person. Once that role no longer exists, in many cases, the chaos of the world is too much for them.

Here's another example: What has Michael Jordan been doing since he retired from the NBA a decade and a half ago? He's been gambling.

Like, a lot.

So much so, in fact, that the media has reported numerous times that he's lost much of what he made playing professional basketball. Fortunately, he still has the endorsement money flowing in, but all of his NBA earnings are apparently gone.

Combining a type A personality with the constant drive to win worked out amazingly well when it had a healthy channel—namely, beating the Detroit Pistons, and pretty much any other team that got in the way. But once that's gone? Type Threes like Jordan still have the drive, but no good outlet for it.

So, if you see him around, give him a hug.

 MANIPULATION
How Threes Impose Their Paradigm on Others

So, how do Type Threes get others around them to affirm the role they've given themselves?

Type Threes want to win, and then **win you over**.

It's like a politician who wants to trounce every other candidate in the primaries… and then seeks out those same candidates to endorse him in the general election.

Again, Type Threes are in the Affinity segment. Belonging is at the core of their desires.

"Beat them until they love you" seems like a strange way to win friends, I know. But all of the Types have a seeming contradiction like this somewhere within their strategies. And if history is any indicator, the Threes present a pretty effective strategy.

Why? Because Types Three and Eight are the ones who keep the world turning. Their collective drive has, from the dawn of time, pushed through the confines of what humans can accomplish. Both Types are powerful, focused, and perpetually aiming at the stars. As opposed to the Type Eights, though, Threes tend to be a lot more likable while they do it.

SPEAKING STYLE
How Threes Communicate with Others

In their effort to win over the hearts and minds of those around them, Threes speak through **propaganda**.

With Threes, everything is a pitch. They are continually selling you something.

Let's say the Three wants to convince his spouse to buy a new car. How's that best accomplished?

Easy. Sit her down after dinner, plug the laptop into the flat screen, and commence with the full-blown sales presentation.

(I'm not joking. I know someone who did this.)

WINGS (W)
The Strategies on Either Side of Type Three

Type Three's wings are **Two and Four**.

3W2 - The Charmer
Here, drivenness meets empathy. The Charmer thrives in networks

where they can lead relationally. You get the social qualities of the Two with the success of the Three. There's a sense of the "razzle-dazzle" with The Charmer. They'll wine and dine you. Warm and charismatic, they're hard not to like.

3W4 - The Professional

The Professional is a bit less gregarious than The Charmer. It's still about succeeding, but it's less relational and more focused on ideas, on building something great.

The Professional tends to be highly ambitious, super creative, and very image-conscious.

COMPLEMENTARY STRATEGIES
The Two Strategies that Round Out Type Three

Type Threes draw their complementary strategies from both Types **Six and Nine**.

Type Threes move *against* others by competing.
Type Sixes move *toward* others for affirmation.
Type Nines move *away* from others for sanctuary.

When operating in health, a Three will pull from the high ends of these two complementaries. In moments of unhealthiness, they draw from the low ends.

When Threes feel secure, they shift into Type Six strategies.

A healthy Three will go to the high side of Six and become loyal to themselves. The Three will also move toward others out of a genuine sense of empathy and compassion.

The unhealthy Three, moving to the low side of Six, will ramp up their own sense of denying reality and do practically anything to achieve their goals, ignoring the consequences completely.

When Threes feel stressed, they reach for the strategies of Type Nine.

A healthy Three, drawing from the high side of Nine, will drop the "mask of success" and begin leading people in a far more genuine way.

When Threes don't feel like they've achieved their goals, they can move to the low side of Nine and become apathetic, despondent, and unfocused.

Why We All Need the Threes

Type Threes get stuff done. And they do it all in style.

Because of that, we look up to Threes. In fact, even Threes look up to Threes.

From kings to professional athletes—and every prominent position in between—history has positioned Threes as the figures most responsible for humanity's milestones. And for good reason: Without Threes, we'd probably still be living in tents made of animal hides and picking our teeth with squirrel bones.

For instance, Augustus Caesar rose from almost total obscurity to become one of the primary architects of the Roman Empire. His main drive? To out-maneuver everyone around him and be adored by the Roman people. He succeeded to the point that upon his death, the Senate bestowed the highest honor possible in both his time and ours. They declared him a god.

Muhammad Ali is also a great example of a Type Three. He wanted to win every battle that presented itself. But merely winning wasn't good enough. He wanted to do it in style. His entire life is a lesson in seizing victory at all costs—and making people love him all the more for it.

Even Andy Warhol serves as a great example of a classic Type Three. He didn't just want to be the most celebrated artist on earth. He sought to redefine *art itself.* But his story is more nuanced than that. All of his attempts at glory stemmed from his desire to bring others along for the ride. More than working just on his own art, he wanted to create a community that worshipped him.

The lesson here is this: We need Threes. And we also need them to live into their strategies. They have a unique set of superpowers necessary for the survival of every single community on earth.

The key, of course, is for Threes to use those superpowers for good.

Because when that happens?

Everyone benefits.

OVERVIEW

Type Three: The Effective Person

Center of Intelligence AFFINITY

Primary Strategy WINNING

Self Image "I AM SUCCESSFUL."

Who's on Your Shoulder THE POLITICAL ADVISOR

Avoidance FAILURE

Fighting Words "YOU ARE A LOSER."

Defense Mechanism IDENTIFICATION

Manipulation WINNING OTHERS OVER

Speaking Style PROPAGANDA

Wings TYPES 2 & 4

Complementary Strategies TYPES 6 & 9

④
TYPE FOUR
The Original Person

I recently saw a clip from Jerry Seinfeld's documentary *Comedian*. A young comic comes up to him backstage and asks, "Jerry, you've made it. You're famous. You had a sitcom. What advice can you give me to achieve those same things, to get to your level?"

Seinfeld looks at the kid and essentially tells him, "If you're going into stand-up comedy looking to get a sitcom, that's not what stand-up is about. I'm a stand-up comedian. We're just not like other people."

Then he tells a story. The Glenn Miller Orchestra was flying to a gig. But because of a snowstorm, they weren't able to land where they needed to. So, the pilot puts the plane down in an icy field, and the musicians have to lug their instruments on foot to the venue.

The musicians are trudging through the snow when they come to a house. Behind a picturesque window, they see a family gathered around a table. The kids are laughing. Everyone is smiling. Grandma and grandpa are there beside a roaring fire. The scene looks like it had been staged by the Hallmark Channel's design department.

After a few moments of looking on at this scene, one miserable musician turns to the other and says, "Man, look at that!"

"Yeah," said the other one, shaking his head. "Yuck. Who would ever want to live like THAT."

That's how Fours view the world.

The Original Person

Type Fours see themselves as *wholly apart* from the rest of us.

Each Four is all alone. The very act of categorizing them is an affront, if only because the primary defining factor of what makes them a Four is that they are, in their own estimation, individually uncategorizable.

It's hard to describe them like that without seeming critical about it. But I'm not. That's how they legitimately view themselves. I know a ton of Fours, and they are AWESOME people. They are just thoroughly convinced, beyond any reasoning with them, that they're different. They feel, at an elemental level, that we cannot feel what they feel. We cannot even begin to fathom the depth of their sadness—or the height of their joy.

And, to be honest, given the quality of the Fours in my life, they may not be wrong. Because, whereas most of the other eight Types are working very hard to avoid pain and suffering, Type Fours—for lack of a better word—*relish it.*

Not that they enjoy pain. Not exactly. They aren't masochists.

They do covet the pain, that's true. But it's not for the pain itself.

It's for what that pain uncovers.

Type Fours have a singular brand of wisdom about reality that, as a non-Four, I am perfectly willing to admit might be superior to the rest of ours in many ways.

They seem to understand two things simultaneously. One, they're cognizant of the scope of all human suffering. And two, in the same breath, they get what it means to rise above that suffering and enter into something cosmically *higher*.

While the rest of us are trying to avoid misery, the Fours not only accept it as a part of the human experience, they expect it as a necessary reality.

I once walked into my former pastor's office and noticed a new wooden sign hanging on the wall. It said, "Happiness is fleeting. It's pain that gives life its meaning."

I asked him where he bought it.

"I didn't," he said. "I made it."

That right there? That's a Four at their most Four-ish.

CENTER OF INTELLIGENCE
The Core Psychological Need of Type Fours

The Type Four is the last of the Hearts from the **Affinity** Center.

Like the Twos and Threes, belonging is (surprisingly!) their primary motive.

I say "surprisingly" because at first glance you wouldn't get it, necessarily. It doesn't make much sense up front. At least it doesn't until you dig a little deeper.

Because, here's the deal...

Type Fours seek to belong above everything else. And to accomplish this, they set themselves apart, view themselves as "other," and keep their distance from the rest of us. Sounds a little nutty, right?

That's perfectly fine in the mind of the Four.

Think of it this way: Let's say Twos, Threes, and Fours are seashells washed up on a beach. Each of these Types within the Affinity section of the Enneagram long for belonging. As seashells, they want beachcombers to come past, see their worth, and pick them up to keep forever.

But, again, their strategies are different.

Twos want to be useful. They want someone to find them and say, "Hey, great! This will make a perfect bottle-opener."

Threes want to be seen as ideal: "This is EXACTLY what a perfect shell looks like!"

And Fours want to be special. They want that beachcomber to look down, see them, and think, "Wow! I've never seen a shell this color before... I'm definitely keeping this one!"

One end goal, three wildly different ways of achieving it: Type Fours don't seek to belong by being either useful or perfect. Instead, they want to cement their value by being the anomaly within the set.

PRIMARY STRATEGY
How Fours Protect Themselves from the Unknown

Type Fours seek to **be unlike anyone else**—and to make themselves essential because of that uniqueness.

I know a Type Four who, in his mid-20s, was convinced he wouldn't live past 30. He wasn't trying to get attention. He honestly thought he was going to die young. (He didn't, but that's beside the point.) The strategies he naturally uses lead him to view himself as "not normal." Type Fours, in their heads, are walking anomalies.

The way they seek to belong is to be nothing like you. Because if they can provide something no one else can, they become indispensable.

SELF-IMAGE
How Fours View Themselves in Light of Their Strategy

"I am special."

Type Fours view themselves as fundamentally different than everyone else on earth. This difference often comes from not having a clear view of who they actually are—their core selves. When they look out into the world, it seems as if they are somehow deficient, as if they lack something essential that everyone else seems to have in spades.

They desire for others to view this deficiency and appreciate them for it. It's like breaking your arm. While the pain and inconvenience aren't fun, at least it's an opportunity to get others to sign your cast.

Fours tend to cultivate a sense of unique beauty. They're into the redemptive power of brokenness, the sublimeness of tragedy.

WHO'S ON YOUR SHOULDER?
The Voice on Repeat Inside a Four's Head

Empowered by embracing pain that makes them uncommon, Fours internalize the voice of a **starving playwright**.

Many Fours turn out to be very talented artists. They believe that their art transcends, and they tend to be unflinching in their desire not to compromise.

Type Fours have a unique (ha!) ability to see pain differently than the rest of us. They see it as temporal, but also find a kind of cosmic grandeur in it. Whereas most of the other Types seek to avoid it altogether, Fours embrace it. They use it. It fuels them.

Not that Fours are entirely morose. Not at all. Along with tragedy, they also adore the comedic. They see the drama on both sides of the continuum. Their only stipulation is that whatever they are experiencing must be both *authentic and transcendent.*

AVOIDANCE
The Thing Fours Must Avoid According to Their Strategy

Type Fours are primarily interested in steering clear of one thing: **normalcy**.

Type Fours are perpetually battling against feeling ordinary. This avoidance happens because once they're ordinary, they feel as though they no longer have anything to offer others.

Which explains, at least in part, why Fours seek belonging by pushing others away. If you've been seeking advice on something and keep hearing the same thing over and over, find a Type Four. They have a talent for approaching scenarios backward and upside down and can provide some great insight into your situation.

Here's another example:

Years back, I was heading up a college ministry called The Well, leading worship and keeping things organized. We'd just gotten new t-shirts, and I wore mine to the next service. Our bassist—a Four— also wore his. I saw him side-eyeing me during setup, but wasn't sure what was going on with him. When we took the stage, I looked over at him again and was surprised to see that he'd changed his shirt. Even within the context of a tightly-knit community, Fours have an unquenchable need to be "original."

Type Fours don't want to ever look like you. Otherwise, they think, they've lost all value to the group.

 FIGHTING WORDS
The Weaponized Language Most Likely to Find Its Way Through the Seams in a Four's Armor

"You are derivative, uninspired, boring, and vanilla."

Just suggesting that a Type Four is anything like anyone else is probably going to force them into the fetal position, at least for a minute or two.

Fortunately, in reaction to your bourgeois patriarchal lack of imagination, they'll soon rouse themselves to go create something that will portray you as a mockery.

And honestly?

It'll probably be pretty great.

DEFENSE MECHANISM
How Fours Reaffirm Their Paradigm to Themselves

Remember that friend of mine who thought he was gonna kick the bucket before his twenties ended? Well, right out of college, he applied to 43 creative writing MFA programs.

(Author's note: That count is exact. He made sure we all knew the precise number.)

Eventually, he got into exactly one graduate program. But before that, as the rejection letters started pouring in, he would hang them on his wall. By the time all of the letters arrived, his room looked like the den of a masochistic madman.

Why display your rejection and disappointment for you and others to be confronted with daily? Because Fours use **introjection** as a defense mechanism.

"Projection" happens when you put your identity onto something outside of yourself. "Introjection," though, is when **you attach something external to your core self**.

Type Fours will collect and display emotional souvenirs. Sometimes those souvenirs will reflect a positive emotion, but most will have deep pain attached to them.

Introjection keeps that pain close so it can help define their uniqueness.

This technique is just more evidence that because Fours feel that they've tapped into the higher "meaning" of pain, they can endure it in the moment.

Another benefit of having Fours in your community stems directly from their tendency to introject. If you're ever going through a tragedy, find someone with strong Four tendencies to sit with you. They'll share your sadness for as long as you need. And then, when the time is right, they'll show you what it really means to sit inside that sadness on a grand—and gloriously transcendent—level.

MANIPULATION
How Fours Impose Their Paradigm on Others

In order to make sure everyone else knows how rare and unique they are, Fours enjoy **being unpredictable**.

Type Fours manipulate others by demonstrating that they approach a subject from a unique angle. And really, they've got this strategy down. If you've been stuck on a problem for a while, find a Four. They will have a different—and potentially more helpful—approach than anyone else you've consulted thus far.

Their whole M.O., again, is to be unpredictable. They may not be overly confrontational about it, but they'll demonstrate their "otherness" nonetheless. And they'll hope you'll love them for it.

(A quick side note: One interesting consequence of having most of the world connected via the internet is that it's growing increasingly harder to maintain that originality. When your primary strategy is to be different than everyone else, that can get hard to manage when a simple social media search reveals whole groups dedicated to exactly what you've previously considered your niche.)

SPEAKING STYLE
How Fours Communicate with Others

The speech of a Four embodies the style, poignancy, and cleverness of **poetry**.

Type Fours have a unique slant on the way they present themselves. Their writing and speaking tend to have a substantive quality.

Other Types use words in utilitarian ways. But for Type Fours, words are just another brush in their studio. If they're not actors or musicians, Fours are often poets or authors.

WINGS (W)
The Strategies on Either Side of Type Four

Type Four's wings are **Three and Five.**

4W3 - The Aristocrat
In this wing, creativity meets determination. People with this wing want as many people as possible to enjoy their art. Bob Dylan isn't just a great songwriter, for example. He's also an entrepreneur.

4W5 - The Bohemian
Originality meets perceptivity. Those with this wing tend to be highly idiosyncratic in their self-expression. Because Type Fives already don't worry too much about what people think about them, adding in the eccentricity of the Type Four tends to result in some pretty atypical approaches to the world.

For example, Salvador Dali was a savant, an artistic genius, and had an anteater as a pet.

COMPLEMENTARY STRATEGIES
The Two Strategies that Round Out Type Four

Type Fours pull strategies from Types **One and Two.**

Type Fours move *away* from others for attention.
Type Ones move *against* others by criticizing.
Type Twos move *toward* others by serving.

At their best, Type Fours go to the high, healthy sides of those two Types. When they aren't especially healthy, they pull from the low ends of those complementaries.

In security, Fours move toward the strategies of Type One.

On the high side of that move, healthy Fours embrace the One's ability to be proactive and move forward to take responsibility and solve problems. They kind of get over themselves and start to get things done.

On the low side of security, though, Fours can get obsessive about recreating their world in the image of their art. They can become workaholics.

Under stress, Fours move to Type Two.

On the high side, instead of navel-gazing, Fours can work to help others and make a real difference in their lives.

At the low end of Two, however, when unhealthy Fours don't feel loved or respected, they can get needy and manipulative.

———————

Why We All Need the Fours

Type Fours give life its flavor. Without them, we'd lose a big part of what makes human culture so vital. Type Ones aren't going to create the Sistine Chapel. Type Twos would never have come up with "Eleanor Rigby." And I dare you to challenge a Three to build a time machine, go back to 19th century Russia and attempt to create something even half as sweeping and soul-stirring as *Anna Karenina*. (The Three will probably try to build the time machine—a challenge is a challenge, after all—but that's about as far as they'll get.)

When Fours accept their "Four-ness," that's when life really starts to get good for the rest of us. We get art. We get culture. We get a way to reframe our lives through the vision of those who feel our shared existence on a level most of us would never get to on our own.

We get the beauty of our world as well as a fresh context for it all.

From Chopin, Tchaikovsky, Edgar Allen Poe, and Virginia Woolf to Bob Dylan, Johnny Depp, and Lady Gaga, Fours create things we've never seen before. They're able to take their pain and synthesize it with what's in the world around them, and then present it to us.

The healthy Four is one of our greatest assets. They're able to humanize us in ways that none of the other Types can manage.

And it's up to the rest of us to honor that desire to remain apart, while still holding them close and making sure they're getting the love and belonging they so desperately need.

After all, we're going to want to see what they'll make next.

OVERVIEW

Type Four: The Original Person

Center of Intelligence	AFFINITY
Primary Strategy	BEING UNIQUE
Self Image	"I AM SPECIAL."
Who's on Your Shoulder	THE STARVING PLAYWRIGHT
Avoidance	NORMALCY
Fighting Words	"YOU ARE BORING & VANILLA."
Defense Mechanism	INTROJECTION
Manipulation	BEING UNPREDICTABLE
Speaking Style	POETRY
Wings	TYPES 3 & 5
Complementary Strategies	TYPES 1 & 2

⑤
TYPE FIVE
The Wise Person

What do Sherlock Holmes, Fox Mulder, Dr. House, and Sheldon from *The Big Bang Theory* have in common?

First, they're not real people.

But secondly—and more importantly—they're all Type Fives.

The Five is your crazy, eccentric genius with the uncanny ability to gather information and put it together into a structured whole.

As I mentioned earlier, I'm a Type Five. But when I first took the Riso-Hudson Enneagram test, I mistyped as a Three. So, when a friend came to me and said, *Nate, bro, I think you're a Five,* I did two things.

First, I told him he was wrong.

Then I went on Amazon and bought ten books on the Enneagram.

Which just proved my Five-ness as nothing else could.

The Wise Person

Personalities in the Identity Center (Types Five, Six, and Seven) are driven by their need for **safety**.

Type Fives do this by withdrawing back into their rich inner world and trying to reestablish their identity and safety.

Their deepest need is safety. And so they gather as much information as they can and attempt to remain unassailable. The idea here is that if I, as a Five, know everything I need to know, there's nothing you can do to undermine that safety.

Like a watchdog in a dark house, Type Fives are continually on the lookout for any potential threats around them. They tend to be junkies for new information. Before they entrust their breakfast to the toaster, they want to know how the thing operates.

They want to know how the world works—everything from the dark mysteries of the cosmos to the inner workings of themselves and their personalities. They're essentially detectives whose *whodunnit* is the universe as a whole.

Type Fives believe, on an essential level, that ultimately they are the only ones they can trust with their safety. That's why they can often come across as standoffish. They aren't intimidated by life, but they are afraid that emotional entanglements will slow them down—and jeopardize their safety.

CENTER OF INTELLIGENCE
The Core Psychological Need of Type Fives

Those in the **Identity** section tend to have a high cognitive intelligence. They're curious, problem-solving folks. They have a "heady" kind of knowing. They seek to be unassailable. Fear is often a powerful negative motivator for them.

Type Fives think themselves through life. And while Sixes and Sevens are also in this slice of the Enneagram and have safety as their primary goal, each approaches the need for security from different angles. Type Sixes achieve that safety by making sure they're on the right team. Type Sevens pour themselves into new experiences. And while Fours are *emotional* black holes—they can't get enough of the feels—Fives are *informational* black holes.

When I tell people that, as a Five, I'm always thinking, scheming, and parsing information, people look at me with some blend of shock and pity. "That sounds exhausting," they say.

For the Type Five, though, it's not exhausting. It's invigorating, in fact. Type Fives run on information in the same way a commercial plane runs on jet fuel.

It's interesting, though. To me, being a Type One and perpetually having to think about how to remain indomitable 24 hours a day, 7 days a week sounds exhausting beyond description. And feeling a Type Two compulsion toward always helping others sounds mind-numbingly *awful*.

Which leads to a truth about the Enneagram Types: To your ears, every one of the other Types' strategies is going to sound, at best, unreasonable, and, at worst, *positively torturous*.

PRIMARY STRATEGY
How Fives Protect Themselves from the Unknown

The Five's primary strategy is **figuring it out**. They only feel safe when they're sure they understand what's happening—and why.

They have the minds of engineers. Understanding the inner workings of things—including themselves—are necessary conditions for their peace of mind.

The idea is this: If they know how everything works, then they'll be prepared for whatever comes their way. And the best way to do that is by observing how everything around—and inside—them works.

SELF-IMAGE
How Fives View Themselves in Light of Their Strategy

"I am perceptive."

While Fives tend to be very intelligent, less brainy Fives also view themselves as being perceptive.

Viewing themselves as an information sponge allows them to feel safe. As long as they know what's going on, they're okay.

Type Fives never want to be caught unawares. Failure for them is being blindsided.

WHO'S ON YOUR SHOULDER?
The Voice on Repeat Inside a Five's Head

Attempting to receive information as objectively as possible, the inner dialogue of a Five is that of a **lab worker**.

Type Fives are fair observers. They have a fantastic, almost Mr. Spockian, ability to gather, store, and analyze information. They're able to run these systems impartially.

Even if the news is terrible, Fives still want to know it. They'll take the hard truth over a pretty lie any day. They just want the information. The data. And often, their reaction to that data isn't (first and foremost, at least) an emotional one.

Type Fives are also amazingly nonjudgmental. You can tell them all sorts of weird things about yourself, and they'll process it with very few motives other than unbridled curiosity.

AVOIDANCE
The Thing Fives Must Avoid According to Their Strategy

Type Fives are constantly fighting a battle against **resource exhaustion**.

Because Fives pursue safety by "figuring it out," they are ultimately trusting their own inner resources to navigate life's craziness. This forces Fives to be very boundaried. They do everything possible to ensure that those internal resources aren't bankrupted.

Many Enneagram instructors confuse this attribute with being introverted. In fact, many Enneagram summaries assume introversion as a part of a Five's checklist. But that's not quite right.

Fives may indeed be introverted, but it's not because the Type's strategy requires it. Fives often opt out of social settings—or say no when asked for help—because they are constantly protecting their internal resources from depletion.

Let's say that it's Christmas morning and your small children
have just opened a toy they're really excited about. But there's one
problem. You didn't notice the "Some Assembly Required" fine print
on the side of the box. As your children open the packaging, you
realize that this toy is going to be fairly complicated to put together.
But your children want to play with it *now,* and they're offering their
enthusiastic help—which you know means the opposite of help,
despite their earnest intentions.

How would you handle that situation?

If you would take the toy into a different room by yourself, lock the
door, read the instructions, and try to assemble it correctly, then
congratulations, you understand a Five's desire to avoid resource
exhaustion. You also probably have a grasp on their defense
mechanism, but we'll get to that in a second.

Fives are boundaried, focused, and intense because they're always
trying to put something together. They're trying to figure it out and
would appreciate it if you kept the noise down in the meantime.

 ## FIGHTING WORDS
*The Weaponized Language Most Likely to Find Its Way
Through the Seams in a Five's Armor*

If you're looking to get a Five's hackles up, just say this:

**"I tricked, duped, and scammed you. You're stupid. You didn't even
see it coming."**

A Five's favorite kind of supervillain is the one who, near the climax
of the story, lays out his whole devious scheme just before the heroes
escape his clutches. (It should also be noted that Fives appreciate

genius wherever they find it. Even in evil schemes.)

Type Fives work very hard to keep from looking dumb—especially when it comes to a subject they feel they should know a lot about.

For example, a Five who makes a living as a plumber is going to know everything about everything when it comes to, say, conduit reamers. He's going to be a genius when it comes to gaskets. His knowledge of pipe extractors could fill the shelves of the Library of Alexandria. Because, if he shows up to a job, doesn't know something, and gets called on it, he's going to implode psychologically.

DEFENSE MECHANISM
How Fives Reaffirm Their Paradigm to Themselves

The Type Five's defense mechanism is **isolation**. This element of their strategy is how they reaffirm their identity to themselves. Again, it's much safer for them to retreat into their heads and run the tests from there.

Related to this strategy is their ability to compartmentalize their lives. Inside the head of a Five are an infinite number of filing cabinets, and only rarely do any of them touch.

For this reason, Fives can come across as intense or detached. They burrow deep into things and work to close the loop on anything they're exploring.

MANIPULATION
How Fives Reaffirm Their Paradigm to Themselves

Type Fives manipulate others by **being preoccupied**. When things start to get sketchy around them, they head for the mental filing cabinets. And when they're processing inside their heads, one of the most annoying things you can do is interrupt them.

Fives send out these "don't interrupt me" signals in pretty overt ways. Last week, for instance, I ate breakfast alone at Bob Evans and kept my earbuds in the whole time. (This did not, however, preclude my genuinely sweet waitress from telling me her life story. Maybe I'll need to get bigger, over-ear headphones for next time.)

If a Five has their door closed, take that as a sign not to bother them. They'll be back out in a bit, just as soon as they have the universe sufficiently figured out—or have, at the very least, replenished their inner resources.

SPEAKING STYLE
How Fives Communicate with Others

The combination of having tons of information stored in their minds and, in many cases, a fairly low ability to pick up on social cues causes Fives to speak in **treatises**.

Type Fives can talk for hours about one subject because they've researched it heavily. If you want to kill an entire afternoon, find a Five and ask them about something they've learned this week. They'll happily oblige.

Type Fives love to teach. To lecture. Part of that motivation is often to establish publicly what they know. But just as often, they simply want to share all the fantastic things they found at the bottom of the research barrel. We all shape our communication style in the way we would like to receive it. For Fives, that means lots of trivia, facts, and lengthy explanations about how and why things work.

WINGS (W)
The Strategies on Either Side of Type Five

The Five's wings are **Four and Six**.

5W4 - The Iconoclast

With "The Iconoclast," curiosity meets individuality. People with this wing enjoy building unique, artful systems from scratch. They rely on implementing processes that can save them time and effort. Because if it works, and it's repeatable, then that structure provides the safety they crave. The Iconoclast is a cerebral, creative, provocative visionary.

5W6 - The Problem Solver

With this wing, observation meets organization. People with this wing process miscellaneous facts to fix things. They tend to be investigative, contrarian, perfection-driven observers.

COMPLEMENTARY STRATEGIES
The Two Strategies that Round Out Type Five

Type Five's complementary strategies pull from Types **Seven and Eight.**

Type Fives move *away* from others for detachment.
Type Sevens move *towards* others for enjoyment.
Type Eights move *against* others by imposing.

At their finest, Type Fives slide to the high, healthy points of those two Types. When they aren't doing well, they slip to the low ends of these same Types.

In security, Fives move toward the strategies of Type Seven.

When a healthy Five moves to Type Seven, they embrace the Seven's ability to be fun and humorous. They move toward others by being quick on their feet and looking for new opportunities to be creative.

On the low side of security and health, though, Fives can get scattered and distracted. If they don't achieve their goals, they can burrow deeper into their mental filing cabinets.

Under stress, Fives move to Type Eight.

Healthy Fives at the high side of Eight don't merely wish to remain hidden and observe, but instead, they jump into life wholeheartedly and "put themselves out there" without fear.

On the low side, however, Fives get aggressive instead of assertive. They tend to isolate themselves even further and adopt a "me against the world" attitude.

Why We All Need the Fives

If the Ones keep us on the straight and narrow, the Twos take care of us, the Threes out-hustle us, and the Fours are working on something impressive, the Fives are here to understand things... and then attempt to communicate their findings to the rest of us.

Some Fives use their insights by looking up: Leonardo Da Vinci, Galileo, Eckhart Tolle, and Thom Yorke from Radiohead have set their sights upon the cosmic, the big picture.

Others, though, have narrowed their gaze down into the fibers of the foundational elements of life itself. Albert Einstein, Stephen

Hawking, Oliver Sacks, and John Nash—just to name a few—are excellent examples of Fives whose curiosity took them down arcane channels into the very essence of things.

While Threes and Eights have tended to be the poster children for historical milestones, Type Fives have often been the driving force behind the most significant shifts in our shared cultural history. While the former two Types might, respectively, sell us the car and drive us around in it, that car wouldn't exist if the Fives hadn't gotten curious, grabbed a socket wrench, and built the thing in the first place.

Within our social fabric, we need Fives to investigate the world around us and report back with their findings. We need them to bear the burden of that constant drive to understand how things work so the rest of us can live into our own skill set.

When Type Fives are at their best, physical and technological progress happens in this world.

So, if you're a Five, grab your tools—whether it's a telescope or a magnifying glass—and get to work. We're all waiting to find out all about your next discovery!

OVERVIEW

Type Five: The Wise Person

Center of Intelligence IDENTITY

Primary Strategy FIGURING IT OUT

Self Image "I AM PERCEPTIVE."

Who's on Your Shoulder THE LAB WORKER

Avoidance RESOURCE EXHAUSTION

Fighting Words "YOU ARE STUPID & UNAWARE."

Defense Mechanism ISOLATION

Manipulation PREOCCUPATION

Speaking Style TREATISE

Wings TYPES 4 & 6

Complementary Strategies TYPES 7 & 8

⑥
TYPE SIX
The Loyal Person

I have a friend who won't buy anything technological that isn't from Apple. I have another friend who would die on a hill defending the superiority of the Android mobile platform.

Here in Ohio, near the end of November, there's an entire week where Ohio State fans won't refer to the University of Michigan by anything but "that team up North." In fact, they'll even actively refuse to use the 13th letter of the alphabet for that time period.

Where I grew up in southeastern Ohio in the foothills of Appalachia, I've seen fistfights break out over the timeless question, "Ford or Chevy?"

I have a cousin who won't touch a Miller Lite with a ten-foot pole. It's Bud Light or die, and he'll declare this unwavering dedication, unprompted, to anyone within earshot.

These acts of allegiance reflect classic Type Six behavior. Seeking safety, they find their refuge within their chosen group. And once they've joined, good luck attempting to get them to change sides.

Like every Enneagram Type, this loyalty can manifest in both terrible and beautiful ways. To illustrate this double-edged sword, you only have to set up all the former Nazi soldiers who later claimed to simply be "doing their jobs" against thousands of Christian martyrs throughout history who would rather die than betray their faith and fellow believers.

For good or for bad, Sixes keep a culture intact.

The Loyal Person

Type Six is called "The Loyal Person" because choosing a side is an enormous part of the Six's strategy. This loyalty can be attached to others, the group at large, or ideas and beliefs. Once forged, this loyalty may never break.

They'll even defend those others—or those beliefs—far more aggressively than they'll defend themselves.

Type Sixes are probably the hardest to pinpoint outside of having them actually take the Enneagram assessment. They're also the hardest to describe. These difficulties arise because the object of their loyalty—people, places, things, ideas, beliefs, just to name a handful—can honestly be *anything*.

What is clear, though, is why they attach themselves so fully to something outside of themselves. Dead set in the Thinking Center of the Enneagram, Sixes struggle with tapping into their inner guide. To deal with the chaos of the world, they tend to put their trust in something external.

They lack self-confidence to the point that while they don't want others deciding for them, they do want to know what the "right answer" is. Coupled with that desire, they also need validation from that surrounding group or belief system.

Which is not to say that they don't think for themselves. They spend *most* of their time thinking, in fact. They are excellent at coming up with worst-case scenarios for any given situation. It should not come as a surprise that Sixes are prone to anxiety.

Many times, that anxiety manifests as a low-level dread that doesn't have anything attached to it. To explain that anxiety, Sixes will create a source. And that source is almost always something that exists outside of the group to which they belong.

Because of this anxiety cycle, Sixes spend most of their time reacting to external stimuli—which is just another reason why they're a little hard to pin down neatly. They tend to react in equal and opposite (and even contradictory) ways depending on what force happens to be exerting the most pressure on them at any given moment.

CENTER OF INTELLIGENCE
The Core Psychological Need of Type Sixes

Type Sixes, as I mentioned earlier, are dead set within the Thinking, or **Identity**, pie slice of the Enneagram. Safety is their primary motivation. Where Type Fives find that safety in hoarding information and Sevens find it by distracting themselves with new experiences, Sixes find safety by fiercely attaching to something external.

Type Sixes will attach to people or groups, of course, but more often this attachment takes the form of an ideology. They need a philosophical system that explains how things work. This system can be as minor as, say, a St. Louis Cardinals fan accepting as gospel the idea that the Cards play the game of baseball *the right way*. It can also be as perilous as someone throwing in their hat with a group of murderous fascists.

It can be as big or as small as you like. The only requisite is that the belief system has to go pretty far in explaining how the world works. And for the Sixes, once they find it, they'll go down with the ship long before ever reexamining that system's validity.

 PRIMARY STRATEGY
How Sixes Protect Themselves from the Unknown

Though it takes many forms, the Six's primary strategy is best summed up in one word: **loyalty**.

It's interesting to note that although the Six is the hardest Type to wrap your head around, a lot of Americans are Sixes. Type Sixes become ardent nationalists, dyed-in-the-wool patriots, stalwart Republicans, to-the-core liberals, hardcore cynics, starry-eyed optimists, fanatical jihadists, and unshakeable evangelicals.

We see so many of these factions clashing each day, it seems, and yet many of the people in these opposing groups are trying to achieve the same thing. They want a system that explains the world. They need a structure that makes sense of the chaos. Their level of devotion is the same. The only difference—and I mean ONLY—is the belief system to which they've (primarily subconsciously) attached themselves.

If that realization doesn't bust open a set of double doors into feeling empathy for people you currently view as "other," I don't know what will.

The next time you watch a debate between members of opposing groups, consider why that debate is even happening. These discussions never change any minds. Most of the time, in fact, the two sides can't even agree on a starting reality. This is not to say the debate shouldn't happen. Of course, it should. But just be aware of what's going on underneath the dialogue next time you stumble into a heated argument.

 SELF-IMAGE
How Sixes View Themselves in Light of Their Strategy

"I am endlessly loyal."

Type Sixes can be excellent troubleshooters... but with a catch. They can figure out problems and propose solutions, but only within the scope of their chosen belief system. Anything that causes even the slightest degree of cognitive dissonance is going to be ignored or explained away.

Unlike Fives, who are objectively analyzing the facts and making decisions based on their discoveries, Sixes are always subjectively critiquing evidence that might upend their most fundamental ideas about the world.

Types Five and Six usually don't make sense to one another, even though they're neighbors on the Enneagram. Type Fives trust only their minds to understand the world. Conversely, Sixes don't trust their perceptions. Because of this doubt, they choose party loyalty to make sure they're safe—a strategy that a Five would utterly disavow.

WHO'S ON YOUR SHOULDER?
The Voice on Repeat Inside a Six's Head

Only ever desiring what's best for their team, the Six's inner voice is that of a **team mascot**, someone who is constantly seeing the best in their own team and finding fault in everyone else.

Type Sixes don't trust themselves to make decisions. As I said before, they subconsciously feel as if they lack some core component for surviving in this world as a human. So, they outsource most of the heavy lifting to their shared ideology.

Everything a Six does is in service to these core beliefs. That said, I do want to make a point here, though: For the sake of clarity, I'm drawing these attachments in very broad strokes. Meaning: Not all Sixes are straight-up fanatics. Some are, of course, but not all.

The strategies used by the Sixes are certainly more nuanced than blindly following their chosen group. They don't want others making decisions for them. Instead, they want to support their communally-held principles, and, in return, have both the belief system and their fellow believers support them.

Type Twos do something similar in their service to others. The difference is that Twos set up this quid pro quo to *belong,* while the Sixes put themselves forward for the "cause" to *remain safe.*

In this quest for safety, Sixes are always attempting to be the most ardent and loyal adherent to whatever ideology they've identified as their team. They support their team in the way they dress, the way they talk, and the way they spend their time and money. They embody their chosen ideology so completely that they seem to be a brand ambassador for the group.

AVOIDANCE
The Thing Sixes Must Avoid According to Their Strategy

Above all, Sixes seek to avoid **rejection** because, if the group kicks them out, there's no safe place to go. The belief system, the group... that's what safety looks like. Lose that alliance, and all is lost.

FIGHTING WORDS
The Weaponized Language Most Likely to Find Its Way Through the Seams in a Six's Armor

As a result of their object of avoidance, to cripple a Six, just repeat after me:

"You've betrayed our ideals. You're excommunicated. Pack your stuff. You're no longer welcome."

They will become completely unmoored.

DEFENSE MECHANISM
How Sixes Reaffirm Their Paradigm to Themselves

How do Sixes reassure themselves that they are on the right team? They use some good, old-fashioned **projection**.

Remember the low-level anxiety I mentioned before? It can be a constant companion for the Six. Because of that nameless dread, Sixes will project their worst fears on to things that the ideology has named as real threats.

You can see this happen with the whole current immigration issue in our country. True or not, many people on the right side of the political continuum project their greatest fears—loss of jobs, loss of safety, loss of what they envision America to be—onto foreigners. So as not to pick on one side and not the other, here's another example. If you ask someone on the left who's responsible for our country's impending doom, they'll identify the other political party, or neo-Nazis, or old white patriarchal men.

Same drive, same problems, same questions... it's only the direct object after the verb that changes.

MANIPULATION
How Sixes Impose Their Paradigm on Others

Type Sixes manipulate others by **testing their loyalty**. Not sure what this looks like? Find any game between the Duke and North Carolina men's basketball teams and watch as the Sixes on each side try to "out-school spirit" their compatriots. The costumes, decorations, full-on face paint... that's less for the opposing team and its fans than it is for their own crew.

SPEAKING STYLE
How Sixes Communicate with Others

Type Sixes speak in **warnings**. They are proactively reactive. They'll complain about the anxiety they feel even while they're using it as fuel to get by each day.

They are always on alert, both for themselves and for others.

WINGS (W)
The Strategies on Either Side of Type Six

The Six's wings are **Five and Seven**.

6W5 - The Defender

Here, loyalty meets problem-solving. People with this wing are apologists for their causes. They are investigating, dependable, contrarian, and can be a bit cynical.

6W7 - The Buddy

Security meets sociability. People with this wing are fun-loving friends you can always depend on. They're reliable, balanced, entertaining, and warm.

COMPLEMENTARY STRATEGIES
The Two Strategies that Round Out Type Six

Type Six's complementary strategies are sourced from Types **Three and Nine**.

Type Sixes move *toward* others for affirmation.
Type Nines move *away* from others for sanctuary.
Type Threes move *against* others by competing.

At their healthiest, the Type Six will pull from the high, healthy ends of these two Types. When things aren't going well, they draw from the low sides of these complementaries.

When feeling secure, a Six will head for the strategies of Type Nine.

At the high side of Nine, a Six's overblown fears will shrink to the proper size. Their attitude will also shift to the positive, harmonious, "it will all work out in the end" perspective of the Nine.

Unhealthy Sixes will move to the low side of Nine to procrastinate and distract themselves by diving deeper into their routines. They become more doubting and will ruminate on problems.

In stressful moments, Sixes move to Type Three.

When a healthy Six pulls from the high side of Type Three, they become productive. They channel their energy into achieving goals and making concrete plans instead of crafting worst-case scenarios and feeling smothered by their fears.

When a Six pulls from the low side of Three, usually because they haven't achieved the safety they desire, they get frantic and busy, which furthers their feelings of being overwhelmed.

Why We All Need the Sixes

Type Sixes are essential to keeping the threads of our social fabric from unraveling. Their loyalty, especially when it's to those around them or noble ideas, is a necessary condition for real cultural change.

From historical figures like Mark Twain, Sigmund Freud, Malcolm X, J. Edgar Hoover, and Richard Nixon to current cultural icons like Spike Lee, Bono, and Rush Limbaugh, Type Sixes will fight tooth and nail for their ideals. They will, without exception, go down with the ship.

They're both the glue and the gears, and when the cause is noble, great things happen. They're hard-working, responsible, and faithful. When something needs to be done for their group, Sixes are the first to volunteer.

When healthy, Sixes can make great leaders. If their social structure has a firm foundation, they will find an exceptional amount of courage to tackle whatever problem presents itself.

Type Sixes are your best teammates, so make sure to offer them some encouragement today. Because, when you need them, they'll be right there for you.

OVERVIEW
Type Six: The Loyal Person

Center of Intelligence IDENTITY

Primary Strategy LOYALTY

Self Image "I AM ENDLESSLY LOYAL."

Who's on Your Shoulder THE TEAM MASCOT

Avoidance REJECTION

Fighting Words "YOU HAVE BETRAYED US."

Defense Mechanism PROJECTION

Manipulation TESTING THE LOYALTY OF OTHERS

Speaking Style WARNINGS

Wings TYPES 5 & 7

Complementary Strategies TYPES 3 & 9

TYPE SEVEN
The Joyful Person

Most of the strategies I employ in my daily life are drawn from Type Five, but I also score pretty high in Type Seven.

As proof, consider this situation in which I found myself recently.

Late one morning, I drove to a town about 15 miles away from where I live. I needed to pick something up and also get out of the office, find a coffee shop, and attempt to get some writing done. I spent a few hours accomplishing these things and started to head back to the office. It was maybe two o'clock in the afternoon at this point.

I then realized something. I didn't want to go back to the office. I wanted to do something fun.

Something fun like... going to see a movie.

The moment the movie idea popped into my head, I did the math.

Factoring in the drive back, I had about two hours before I'd be expected to be home to help my wife with our three kids and get dinner fixed.

The numbers didn't appear to work in my favor. Even still, I checked the movie times. More bad news. I could've seen a movie, but I wouldn't have gotten back by four, for sure.

I ran the scenarios. If I showed up 45 minutes later than normal, my wife was going to be mad. But how mad? Like, really mad? Or, like, *totally-worth-seeing-a-movie-anyway* mad?

It basically came down to this: There was no way I was going to be able to sell my wife on the idea that I was knocking off work early, going to see a movie alone, and would be getting home way later than I should. Even bringing up the idea would likely start a fight.

Plus, the responsible thing to do in the situation would be to either go back to the office or go home. People in both of those places were expecting me to do things that afternoon.

I knew all of this information—I was conscious of each and every part of it—even while I was driving to *the movie theater.*

I got as far as the parking lot before coming to my senses and turning back onto the highway to head back home. Responsibility, for at least that afternoon, won out.

The difference between me and a strong Seven?

The Seven will always go see the movie.

———————

The Joyful Person

You probably have at least one friend who's a Seven. They are the ones who are essentially down for whatever adventure arises.

Leaving for a last minute road trip? They're in.

Want to enter a doubles badminton tournament? They're game.

Jonesing to try the gelato place that just opened up four towns over and need a partner-in-crime? They're already in the car with the engine running.

Type Sevens are busy. They can be very productive. They make a lot of plans. They're enthusiastic about having new experiences. They are the life of the party, no matter what kind of party it is.

Type Sevens are often adventure junkies. They are endlessly chasing real, immersive adventures to avoid pain and remain unassailable.

You want Sevens in your life. They are, put simply, *fun*.

Type Sevens are quick on their feet. They're hard to pin down—and this constant duck-and-weave is by design. Type Sevens don't want to feel pain. And the hardest target to hit is a moving one.

CENTER OF INTELLIGENCE
The Core Psychological Need of Type Sevens

Type Sevens, like the Fives and Sixes, are in the **Identity** section of the Enneagram. But where Fives seek safety by hoarding the raw data of life, and Sixes look for safety in ideologies, Sevens tend to deal with the chaos of life by working to stay on the move, distracted, immersed.

It's interesting: Many Sevens feel safer standing at the edge of a cliff than they do alone with their own thoughts. Because those thoughts might cause them pain, they are far more comfortable facing a physical void than they are an internal, psychological one.

Or, think of it this way: Sevens feel as if they lack identity. They have a deficit of what could be described as a "safety of the self." To compensate, they are perpetually driven to push in directions that the rest of us would likely consider very *unsafe*. New ideas generate new experiences, and those experiences produce new ideas. The more intense the experience, the better a distraction it is. Engaging in this cycle allows the Seven to forget about the underlying anxiety that fuels them.

Type Sevens are great at coming up with new ideas, or pulling existing ideas together. Their minds are endlessly and proactively reaching for whatever new information might be available in the next breath. In general, Type Sevens aren't bookish or endowed with excellent study habits. Instead, because they are such quick learners, they tend to be the kind of folks who cram for a few hours just before the exam and come out among the top performers in the class.

Sounds great, right? From the description thus far, you might get the notion that being a Seven is all sunshine and roses. And being a Seven is great. But there are undoubtedly some downsides to this strategy as well.

For one, chasing the next thrill tends to lead you to some pretty dangerous spots. Base-jumping is fun, I'm sure, but the margins for error aren't exactly in your favor. The attractive thing about risky behavior (especially for the Seven) is that there's a chance you could die. The bad thing about risky behavior? See above. You could die.

This illustration is obviously an extreme example. But even bringing it back down to earth a bit, Sevens have other challenges beyond risking life and limb.

They tend not to plan for the future, focusing instead on either what they're doing right this moment or what fun thing they're heading out to next. They're more inclined to avoid things that cause pain than face them head-on.

Responsibilities aren't fun. Type Sevens know it.... and tend to act accordingly.

It's very easy for Sevens to slip into a mode of tuning out any negative signals coming from inside them, whether those are psychological, emotional, or spiritual. It's also easy for Sevens to fall into selfish patterns, focusing more on what they need than what others might need from them. They can be childish, irresponsible, and utter slaves to their passions.

But, again... it's that double-edged sword making its entrance once more. Type Sevens are like little kids—with all the attendant blessings and challenges. As with all the other Types, a healthy Seven is a balanced one.

PRIMARY STRATEGY
How Sevens Protect Themselves from the Unknown

Type Seven's main strategy is to **enjoy life to the fullest**.

Driven by the need for identity, safety is their biggest concern.

They are endlessly chasing new experiences in an effort to remain unassailable. They are perpetually on the lookout for the next fun thing they can do in order to avoid negativity.

SELF-IMAGE
How Sevens View Themselves in Light of Their Strategy

"I am happy."

Type Sevens are some of the best people to have around during a disaster. They are bent on making the best of a dire situation. The eternal optimists, if you ask them how they're feeling on a scale of one (super bad) to ten (super great), they will rarely give you a number lower than six.

You only have $20 in your bank account until next week? Great! Let's have a ramen noodle feast!

Your car broke down on the highway in a rainstorm, and your cell phone is dead? Awesome. Let's find some makeshift ponchos and go for a seven-mile hike to the closest service station!

Type Sevens view themselves as happy. Anything less than happiness is a total disaster (which they may still attempt to spin into the first line of their next adventure story).

WHO'S ON YOUR SHOULDER?
The Voice on Repeat Inside the Seven's Head

Sevens believe their role is to ensure that everyone is always having a good time. Because of this, their inner world has the vibe of a **cruise ship director**.

Type Sevens are constantly looking for fun, for the next adventure. Again, their mental energy is spent looking for *what's next*.

Type Sevens tend to be extroverted, warm, friendly, and adventure-seeking. Combine all those things and you have the kind of people who are great at planning sublime excursions and organizing group events. They always have something going on, and they're more than willing to bring their friends—or perfect strangers, for that matter!—along with them.

 ## AVOIDANCE
The Thing Sevens Must Avoid According to Their Strategy

Type Sevens seek to avoid **pain**.

Type Sevens are looking for safety. Their internal struggle with identity flows directly from—like all three Types within the Cognitive section—being out of touch with their inner guide.

By focusing on enjoying life to the fullest, they're able to give order to the chaos of the world and avoid the danger of the "internal unknown."

 ## FIGHTING WORDS
The Weaponized Language Most Likely to Find Its Way Through the Seams in a Seven's Armor

"You are such a drag."

If you want to spoil a Seven's morning, just tell them that they're no fun. Type Sevens pride themselves on keeping the party going. Any hint that they're not fulfilling this part of their self-appointed destiny is sure to bring them down.

But, keep this in mind…

They won't be down for long. They might mope a bit, but in no time they're going to be back at it, sussing out where the next adventure is going to take them—and remaining confident that they'll be able to convince you to come along.

 ### DEFENSE MECHANISM
How Sevens Reaffirm Their Paradigm to Themselves

As their defense mechanism, Sevens use **sublimation**, which is just a fancy word for finding the silver lining in every rain cloud.

The idea here is that if even the worst things can have a positive spin, then no situation is a complete and total tire fire.

Got fired from your job? No problem. That just opens up your week for another adventure.

Won the lottery but then ran the ticket through the wash? It's all good. That much money would have ruined all your close relationships anyway.

Lost your keys? Whatever. It's a nice day for a walk. Who cares if it's ten below outside?

Type Sevens don't just roll with the punches. They make a game out of every jab.

 ### MANIPULATION
How Sevens Impose Their Paradigm on Others

Type Sevens put their own paradigm on others by **distracting** them.

I used to have a Type Seven on my staff. Every Monday we'd have a staff meeting, and he was good for about an hour or so before you could tell he was done digging into the dry administrative stuff.

He never did it consciously, but just like clockwork, right at the one-hour point, something would remind him of a story, which would then remind him of another story. Pretty soon the meeting was completely off course. It was like a real life *If You Give a Mouse a Cookie* scenario. Which was fine. His stories were great. (This situation forced me to learn how to pack a ton of necessary talking points into a much shorter meeting, which made for a happier staff.)

But the manipulation strategy is there. As a Seven, he gets bored, and the best way to remedy the situation is to bring others along with him in his escape.

 SPEAKING STYLE
How Sevens Communicate with Others

Type Seven's speaking style is **storytelling**. They are continually creating narratives that pull others into their orbit. In fact, whenever something bad happens, one of the first things a Seven tells herself is, "At least this will make a good story somewhere down the line."

Take the worst thing in the universe, and the Seven, when communicating it to you, will put as positive a spin on it as possible. They want to bring you along, to get you on board. And the best way to do that, according to their primary strategy, is to build an amazing scenario and draw you in.

This process reinforces their Defense Mechanism of sublimation. Every epic story has to have some difficult parts, but Sevens want you to know that ultimately there will be a happy ending.

WINGS (W)
The Strategies on Either Side of Type Seven

The Seven's wings are **Six and Eight**.

7W6 - The Entertainer

Playfulness meets productivity. People with this wing are the life of the party, wherever they go. They are spontaneous, quick, gregarious, and impulsive. They are perpetually driven both to dream big and engage with others.

7W8 - The Realist

Adventuring meets forcefulness. People with this wing are determined to get what they want out of life. They are extroverted, engaged, prone to impatience, and tend to attempt to escape into whatever experience presents itself.

COMPLEMENTARY STRATEGIES
The Two Strategies that Round Out Type Seven

For complementary strategies, Sevens turn to Types **Five and One**.

Type Sevens move *toward* others for enjoyment.
Type Fives move *away* from others for detachment.
Type Ones move *against* others by criticizing.

At their healthiest, Type Sevens will channel the high, healthy ends of these two Types. In unhealthy moments, they head to the low sides of these complementaries.

In security, Sevens head to the strategies of Type Five.

A healthy Seven will go to the high side of Five to get some needed distance from their hectic life and reflect on life's essentials. Here, they put their nose to the grindstone and get things done.

An unhealthy Seven, however, shifts to the low end of Type Five, becoming even more detached from reality and increasingly enamored with their dreams and plans.

Under stress, Sevens pick up the strategies of Type One.

A healthy Seven can go to the high side of One to become more focused and disciplined. Here they find balance by doing what they *need* to do now and put off what they *want* to do until later.

Stressed Sevens, when unhealthy, go to the low side of One. After being unable to achieve their goals, Sevens can become angry and resentful, blaming others for not giving them that to which they feel entitled. In this frustration, they put the cause of their disappointment on others.

Why We All Need the Sevens

Here's a story that perfectly encapsulates why we need Type Sevens in our social orbit:

A psychiatrist had twin sons. One was a pessimist. The other was an optimist. On their birthday, he decided to run a little experiment.

He put all the presents in the pessimist's room and put his name on all the tags. In the optimist's room, he dumped several wheelbarrows' worth of horse manure.

When he walked into their rooms that morning, the pessimist was sitting on the floor crying.

"What's wrong?" the father asked.

"I've got to find a bunch of batteries to get these toys to work. Then I have to figure out how to play all these new video games. Plus, I got so much stuff that it's not all going to fit on my shelves!"

When the father found his optimistic son, however, the boy looked overjoyed.

"Why are you so happy?" he asked his son.

"Dad, just look at all this horse poop! There's gotta be a pony around here somewhere!"

That joke is a great example of what it means to be a Type Seven. They make the best of a (literally) crappy situation. From Mozart, Thomas Jefferson, Benjamin Franklin, and Amelia Earhart all the way over to James Franco and Miley Cyrus, Sevens throughout history have been primarily engaged in pouring themselves into whatever adventure they can find—and having a blast doing it.

Find the Sevens in your life today, figure out what they're doing, and then jump into it with them. I promise you won't be sorry!

OVERVIEW
Type Seven: The Joyful Person

Center of Intelligence IDENTITY

Primary Strategy ENJOY LIFE

Self Image "I AM HAPPY."

Who's on Your Shoulder THE CRUISE SHIP DIRECTOR

Avoidance PAIN

Fighting Words "YOU ARE SUCH A DRAG."

Defense Mechanism SUBLIMATION

Manipulation DISTRACTION

Speaking Style STORYTELLING

Wings TYPES 6 & 8

Complementary Strategies TYPES 5 & 1

(8)
TYPE EIGHT
The Powerful Person

My younger brother Levi and I grew up in the southeastern corner of Ohio. When I was around 16— Levi would've been 13 or so—he and I drove to a high school basketball game a few towns over. We went to hang out with one of my friends who attended that school.

As we were sitting in the stands, a few kids came over and started picking on my friend. I wasn't sure what to do, so I stood up and told the other kids to leave my friend alone. I wasn't aggressive about it, but my intervening still managed to ratchet up the tension.

So, now we were in this argument. I was just about to grab my friend and urge him to move to another part of the gym. Before I could get his attention, though, I saw a flash of something in the corner of my eye. The next thing I knew, one of the bullies was on the ground holding his eye. Levi stood over him, fists clenched.

Levi nodded at me and walked away. The time for talking, at least for Levi, was over. All of a sudden it was time to get out of there... and quickly.

It wasn't until years later, when I was first introduced to the Enneagram, that I realized what had happened in that moment.

Levi was (and is still) an Eight.

And Eights are always up for a fight.

The Powerful Person

I appreciate Type Eights for a number of reasons, but at the top of the list is this: Of all the Types, the Eights' motivations are clearly evident in whatever situation they find themselves.

They're a lot of things. But *mysterious* isn't one of them.

Type Eights want power. They want control. No matter what their job is—from dictator to Uber driver—they want to have the first and final say in what happens around them.

Their primary strategy is to *fight*.

Although my eldest child Rosie is only four—and a bit young to be wrung through the Enneagram assessment process—she often displays the tendencies of an Eight, making parental duties far more adventurous than they otherwise would be. I love her with every ounce of my being. I also appreciate that no one is ever going to successfully take advantage of her in any way. But, man, that girl certainly makes life *interesting*.

Here's the primary thing that I've learned about Eights firsthand:

You will never win with them.

You know how in a disagreement, when things get heated, one person is able to go up to that next level, and the other person backs off because it becomes too much for them?

Yeah. That will never happen with an Eight. It's as if they have Tom Petty's song "I Won't Back Down" playing on repeat in their heads 24/7. They seem to lack the little warning gauge the rest of us have in our brains that flashes red when things have gone TOO FAR. In its place, they have an unending source of psychic fuel that allows them to continue to go higher and higher, *ad infinitum.*

And then... even if you do manage to win? It's not a true victory.

If I get Rosie to finally put her socks on, her angle shifts, she goes into full historical revisionist mode, and she'll announce that socks were her idea in the first place and, besides, she wanted to put them on anyway.

I'm like 400% bigger than her, and it still never feels like a fair fight.

 CENTER OF INTELLIGENCE
The Core Psychological Need of Type Eights

We're back to the **Autonomy** Center, where we started with Types Eight, Nine, and One.

In this slice of the Enneagram pie, these three Types' primary need in life is to **maintain control over their fate**. They have highly attuned instinctual survival skills. They depend heavily on their "gut knowledge." They seek to be unbeatable, and anger can be a useful tool to that end.

Whereas Ones seek that control through obeying the rules and Nines try to find it by searching for peace, Type Eights are self-confident, powerful, and forceful in their attempt to keep control of their lives.

Their instincts work in pretty straight lines. If there's a threat, they seek to eliminate it. If something is standing between where they are now and where they want to go, they will move that obstacle out of the way.

They are stolid individualists and will work very hard not to be indebted to anyone else.

PRIMARY STRATEGY
How Eights Protect Themselves from the Unknown

Eights have the most straightforward approach of any Enneagram Type. In order to ensure that they are never coerced into anything, Eights **fight hard for their own way**.

The Eights impose their will on others to fulfill their desire to bring their lives under control. They use their power and resiliency to ensure their autonomy.

Again, you see the straight lines in their strategy. There's a threat. That threat needs to be removed. And the Eight is going to fight tooth and nail to crush that threat and take back control of their lives and the world around them.

SELF-IMAGE
How Eights View Themselves in Light of Their Strategy

"I am strong."

They are physically and emotionally tough. Type Eights can, by nature, endure a lot. In their quest to keep from being hurt emotionally, they'll let the world pound at their outer defenses for much longer than most of us could stand. They'll choose pain over the loss of their autonomy all day long.

If you watch an Eight, you'll see that they physically take up a lot of space. They tend to spread out and take up more room than non-Eights. A lot of their mannerisms are (subconsciously) aggressive. Everything about them is, well, *intense.*

WHO'S ON YOUR SHOULDER?
The Voice on Repeat Inside an Eight's Head

Eights don't tolerate weakness, least of all in themselves. The voice in their head is akin to a **drill sergeant** barking out bombastic and intense commands. Some version of the phrase, "Suck it up, buttercup!" is stuck on repeat in their mental playlist.

Type Eights are constantly reasserting their strength. Their indomitability. Their power.

They are always pushing themselves to get things done in incredible quantities, but often to the detriment of their relationships. They tend to lack empathy for others, primarily because they don't allow themselves to feel much empathy for themselves.

There is one exception, though. They tend to have tons of empathy for people they perceive as weak and in need of protection. This need to defend others stems from their incredibly visceral sense of justice. They are perpetually primed to defend others they perceive as vulnerable, including animals, because of this strong sense of justice.

For people whom they perceive as equal or superior, though? The amount of empathy they harbor for them, almost across the board, is going to come up double zeroes.

AVOIDANCE
The Thing Eights Must Avoid According to Their Strategy

Type Eights seek to avoid **vulnerability** at all costs. Very few people will ever really know an Eight on a deep level. I've heard it said that, for Eights, they might open up to one, maybe two people during their *entire lives*. Their armor is grafted onto their skin. And even then, when they do let those select few inside, there's still a couple of impenetrable inches remaining between the outside world and their inner self.

FIGHTING WORDS
The Weaponized Language Most Likely to Find Its Way Through the Seams in an Eight's Armor

Want to start a fight with an Eight?

It's not super hard, as you might imagine.

Something simple like, "Wanna fight?" ought to do the trick.

Need something more specific? Try this:

"Everybody knows that you're incompetent and weak. You don't think we know it, but we do."

Type Eights can't bear the idea of someone taking advantage of them. They loathe the idea of being scammed. Anything that impedes their autonomy is going to walk away, at a bare minimum, with a metaphorical (and sometimes literal) black eye.

DEFENSE MECHANISM
How Eights Reaffirm Their Paradigm to Themselves

Eights don't believe in showing weakness, so they just act like they don't have any. They reaffirm their power to overcome any obstacle through **denial**. Imagine the Black Knight in *Monty Python and the Holy Grail* having both arms and legs chopped off while insisting, "It's only a flesh wound."

Type Eights have the most transparent strategy to get what they want, but also tend to have the hardest time engaging in reality. If you continuously tell yourself—and others—that you're the toughest person alive, human nature tends to lend itself to believing that myth at some point.

The truth, for the Eight, tends not to matter nearly as much as the result. Most anything can justify the means to victory.

Naturally, while history is full of monsters who were most definitely strong Eights, very few Eights are exclusively using Eight strategies. So the "win at all costs" strategy tends to get a little tamped down by both the wings and the complementary strategies.

If you find someone in power who seems like a bully, has (at minimum) a strained relationship with clear and indisputable facts, and tends to be comfortable with calling the sky purple in one moment and then denying ever having said such a thing in the next, you're looking at an Eight. (An unhealthy Eight, for sure, but an Eight just the same.) Along with all the other characteristics of a classic Eight, you'll see just how much they can come to depend on denial for maintaining control over the chaos of life.

But, again, that tool can be put to really positive use as well. The Eights are the hardest to get along with of the nine Types, but they also tend to bear much of the load for what gets done down here on earth. They're movers and shakers. They're willing to make the hard decisions. They topple dynasties and build empires out of the ashes. Healthy Eights are incredible assets to everyone around them. Like the wolves in Yellowstone, they are majestic, aggressive, glorious, savage, and absolutely essential for the ecosystem to function.

MANIPULATION
How Eights Impose Their Paradigm on Others

Type Eights **dominate** others. That's how they assert—or, more accurately, *impose*—their paradigm on the rest of us.

They want what they want, and if you're standing in their way, there's going to be conflict.

Put it this way: Type Eights have never met a door they're not eager to kick down.

SPEAKING STYLE
How Eights Communicate with Others

Just like every other aspect of a Type Eight, their speaking style is very clear and direct. They give **commands** and expect to be obeyed.

Type Eights don't have much time for finesse. After all, they have their whole reality to maintain with white-knuckled fervor. So, when they want something done, they're going to get to the point and tell you exactly what you need to do. Why use six words when three will get the job done?

WINGS (W)
The Strategies on Either Side of Type Eight

The Eight's wings are **Seven and Nine.**

8W7 - The Independent
Authority meets charisma. People with this wing exude great self-confidence and love to lead others. The "Independents" seek power and look to revolutionize systems. They are rebels at heart.

8W9 - The Bear
Power here meets perspective. People with this wing display a grounded quality that inspires and awes others. They tend to lead, challenge, and delegate, but can also be so territorial that they slip into patterns of bullying.

COMPLEMENTARY STRATEGIES
The Two Strategies that Round Out Type Eight

For their complementary strategies, Eights go to Types **Two and Five**.

Type Eights move *against* others by imposing.
Type Fives move *away* from others for detachment.
Type Twos move *toward* others by serving.

At their best, Type Eights pull from the high, healthy ends of these two Types. When they aren't especially healthy, they pull from the low ends.

In security, Eights move to Type Two's strategies.

At the high side of Two, healthy Eights combine empathy with power and use their energy to build up the broader community rather than merely defend their position.

On the low side of Two, Eights become intentional enablers who want people to depend on them as a means of further manipulation and control.

Under stress, Eights reach for the strategies of Type Five.

At the high, healthy side of Five, Eights become detached and objective. This shift allows them to reflect dispassionately and make a wiser choice on how to proceed.

However, on the low, unhealthy side of Five, after not being able to achieve their goals, Eights retreat into their minds to sulk, blame others, and plot revenge.

Why We All Need the Eights

A few months back I uncovered a fascinating story about Winston Churchill, a classic Eight if there ever was one.

Near the end of World War II, the Nazis had taken control of Paris and were prepared to take over the full French Navy fleet—which would've spelled doom for the British once and for all. France and Britain had a long-standing agreement that if France came under Nazi control, France would destroy their ships to keep them out of enemy hands. But, now that that exact situation had reared its ugly head, the French captains refused to destroy their ships.

Caught in a no-win situation, Churchill did what he thought was best. He gave the command, and a fleet of British ships bombed the French vessels into oblivion.

It's not nice. It won't leave you unchanged. But sometimes it's necessary.

That's the burden that Eights eternally bear. And when that willingness to make the hard calls stems from the desire to better the lives of others, there's no more powerful force for good within humanity's ranks.

You can see this in the lives of historically famous Eights like Franklin D. Roosevelt, Martin Luther King Jr., and Oskar Schindler. They stand up for what they believe, and nothing short of death is going to stop them.

An unhealthy Eight is a disaster just waiting to happen.

But a healthy Eight? They have the drive and ability to terraform the globe into a paradise for *them* to rule... and for the rest of us to enjoy.

OVERVIEW

Type Eight: The Powerful Person

Center of Intelligence AUTONOMY

Primary Strategy FIGHT FOR THEIR WAY

Self Image "I AM STRONG."

Who's on Your Shoulder THE DRILL SERGEANT

Avoidance VULNERABILITY

Fighting Words "YOU ARE WEAK."

Defense Mechanism DENIAL

Manipulation DOMINATION

Speaking Style COMMANDS

Wings TYPES 7 & 9

Complementary Strategies TYPES 2 & 5

⑨
TYPE NINE
The Peaceful Person

One of the craziest stories I remember being told by one of my professors back in college started out as a discussion about a collection of short stories he was writing.

Just as an offhand comment, he'd mentioned something about certain stories based on his family that he could never put into a work of short fiction.

"Oh," I said. "Because it would be embarrassing for your family if you publicized it?"

"Oh, no," my professor replied. "It's because if I wrote it even remotely close to how it happened in real life, it wouldn't make it past any fiction editor in the world. It would be completely unbelievable. No one would ever be able to imagine that happening in real life."

He then told me the story. And... he was right. If I didn't know how forthright a guy he was, I wouldn't have believed it either.

So, from what I gathered from the several classes I had with him, my professor's extended family seemed to be pretty dysfunctional. But every relationship in that family tree looked like June and Ward Cleaver compared to one particular couple.

My professor wasn't sure what had happened, but there had been a dispute between his aunt and uncle a few decades before. Apparently, it was a significant dispute. But instead of working it out, or even getting a divorce, they chose a third, mind-bendingly avoidant path.

For over 40 years, they did not speak one word to one another.

Not one.

They continued to live together, do their daily routines, live as otherwise completely regular people. Except for, you know, not talking to each other at all—or even acknowledging that the other person existed.

That, of course, is an extreme example. (I'm not sure I can even imagine how that would work on a practical, daily level.) But if I had to put a number on the aunt and uncle, they would definitely be Type Nines.

Radically unhealthy Nines, yes. But Nines nonetheless.

The Peaceful Person

The Type Nine tends to be relaxed, easy going, and will go to great lengths to avoid conflict. They are usually artistic, positive, and helpful, but they can also fall into the trap of going along with others to avoid conflict.

Type Nines are addicted to smooth sailing. They want everything around them to be peaceful, whether that's a healthy or unhealthy homeostasis. They also want everything inside them to be at peace. The monster in their closet at night goes by the name Friction; under the bed lives Discord.

They can be too willing to follow the status quo, or minimize real problems by shrugging them off or attempting to ignore them. Ostriches are Nines.

They can be passive and stubborn (especially when challenged directly). But at their best they can be powerful, rational, empathetic peacemakers who can bring opposing sides together and help heal conflicts.

 ### CENTER OF INTELLIGENCE
The Core Psychological Need of Type Nines

Here's why I love the concept of the Centers of Intelligence:

Take a look at Type Eight and Type Nine—next door neighbors, up there for life.

Now, if you put an Eight and a Nine in a lab and run the same diagnostics under the same conditions, you would discover that they are almost exactly the opposite of one another.

But here's the thing. They're not just side by side on the Enneagram. They're actually in the *same Center of Intelligence*. Which means two things. One, their strategies come from the same place—that instinctual, heightened lizard-brain knack for survival. And two, they actually want the *exact same thing!*

It's the literal embodiment of fight versus flight.

As members of the **Autonomy** Center, Nines want control of their future, their fate.

But while Eights seek to achieve that by fighting tooth and nail for every scrap of independence, and Ones try to remain invincible through strict adherence to the rules, Nines sort of just want to be left to their own devices. They avoid conflict like the plague.

This, of course, is a double-edged sword—and the plague analogy is apt.

Sometimes, it's a good idea to avoid the plague. It has its benefits. You continue to survive, you're free of crippling, possibly fatal symptoms, and you don't become a disease vector yourself.

On the other hand, sometimes plagues need intervention. They often don't stop spreading until someone takes up the cause, figures out what needs to happen to contain it, and then makes the hard decisions to stop it altogether by facing the issue head-on.

So, for the Nine, it's important for them to understand when to fly—as well as when to fight. But given the choice? It's flight almost every time.

PRIMARY STRATEGY
How Nines Protect Themselves from the Unknown

Type Nines' primary strategy is **cultivating harmony**. They want peace, serenity, and unity.

The thinking is this: "You can't make me do anything I don't want to do if I always just concede to doing *what you want to do.*"

This wet noodle of a strategy isn't what happens all the time, of course. They aren't necessarily chickens, or pushovers. But their default setting is going to be more rainbow trout and less sockeye salmon.

In their minds, *just playing along* is usually the best way to get that autonomy they want most.

I don't usually take a lot of my wisdom from horror-movie tropes, but when I do, I make them count. You'll notice that between an Eight and a Nine, when confronted with some maleficent entity threatening their lives at an abandoned campground, the Eights are the ones who get out of the tent to look. The Nines, on the other hand, just play dead. More often than not, they both die... but at least the Nine gets to go second.

 SELF-IMAGE
How Nines View Themselves in Light of Their Strategy

"I am content."

Jeff Bridges's character "The Dude" in *The Big Lebowski* is a great example of a Type Nine. Throughout the film, crazy, intense stuff continues to happen, and while he starts to lose his zen in a few isolated moments, he mostly just handles it all with a calm aplomb that most of us would never be able to muster.

So, let's put it this way:

The Nines *abide.*

WHO'S ON YOUR SHOULDER?
The Voice on Repeat Inside the Nine's Head

Desiring to sow seeds of peace wherever they go, the Nine's inner voice is that of a **mediator**.

The inner dialogue for a Nine tends toward the spiritual, the interconnected. They tend to be a little cosmic in their self-talk.

They are also incredibly nonjudgemental, which makes other people love to be around them.

The Nine sits on top of the Enneagram and just observes. They are great at seeing all sides of an issue. And the fact that they are so nonjudgmental means that people tend to seek them out for advice, wisdom, or just a listening ear.

AVOIDANCE
The Thing Nines Must Avoid According to Their Strategy

Type Nines seek to avoid **conflict**.

Type Nines hate friction. They absolutely hate it. I've known Nines that would rather chew off a limb than have a hard conversation.

Why? Because it all gets back to autonomy. When in conflict, they fear that something is going to be taken away, that they're going to lose something essential to their freedom.

Whereas the Eights relish the idea of hitting this potential roadblock head-on, Nines often can't handle both the internal and external negative feelings that might result.

For Nines, how others view them is either liberating or imprisoning. It's liberating when they're surrounded—inside and out—by positive vibes. It's imprisoning when the frequencies shift into the red.

What's interesting here, though, is that when you directly challenge their autonomy, they can be immovable in their stubbornness. They'll avoid conflict as much as they can, but push them into a spot where their freedom is at stake, and they'll fight you as aggressively as an Eight. Again, remember that their primary goal in life is to maintain control of their future. Like raccoons, they'll avoid most direct conflict, skittering away into the shadows of a storm drain when you get close. But if you get them into a corner and there's no perceived escape, out come the teeth and claws.

With Nines, you have to take Bruce Lee's advice: Be like water. You move slowly around them and they'll let you pass every time. But go at them hard, like smacking the surface of a stream with your palm, and they aren't going to *bend,* let alone break.

FIGHTING WORDS
The Weaponized Language Most Likely to Find Its Way Through the Seams in the Nine's Armor

"You're a bully. You always want your way."

Say that to a Nine and you'll break their will... at least until they take the first opportunity to ignore you altogether.

DEFENSE MECHANISM
How Nines Reaffirm Their Paradigm to Themselves

Type Nines reaffirm their paradigm to themselves by a process we call **narcotization.** They seek peace and escape, and that can take the form of anything that's both immersive and distracting. This can run the gamut between spending a lot of time alone on a hobby to slipping into drug addiction.

The object can be anything. But it usually becomes something they continually return to.

MANIPULATION
How Nines Impose Their Paradigm on Others

Nines impose their paradigm on others by **tuning out external expectations.** If they feel like they can't live up to others' expectations, they are adept at simply ignoring them.

This works on the positive side as well. If someone's expectations are very low for a Nine, they are able to seize the opportunity and confidently pursue their goals unencumbered.

SPEAKING STYLE
How Nines Communicate with Others

Other Enneagram experts write about the Nines' speaking style as a grand story, where they craft this massive epic that they can lose themselves inside.

I disagree.

Instead, the Nine's speaking style is **de-escalation.**

They're always diffusing, always trying to put out the little fires popping into existence around them.

I am a Five and my brother is an Eight. When we're together, it's like oil and water (or, perhaps, oil and fire). So my mother, the Nine, spends most of these family get-togethers mediating, de-escalating, and, in general, keeping the peace. She's achieved a moderate level of success down through the years.

WINGS (W)
The Strategies on Either Side of Type Nine

The Nine's wings are **Eight and One**.

9W8 - The Referee
Gentleness meets endurance. People with this wing work to provide meditation and lessen conflicts. They tend to be good negotiators, optimistic, inspiring, and also, sometimes, a bit belligerent.

9W1 - The Dreamer
Acceptance meets purpose. People with this wing can synthesize diverse perspectives into an ideal vision. They are independent peacemakers, philosophical, and stubborn when pushed.

COMPLEMENTARY STRATEGIES
The Two Strategies that Round Out Type Nine

Type Nines pull their complementary strategies from **Three and Six**.

Type Nines move *away* from others for sanctuary.
Type Sixes move *toward* others for affirmation.
Type Threes move *against* others by competing.

At their finest, Nines pull from the high, healthy ends of these two Types. At their worst, they pull from the low ends.

In security, the Nine chooses the strategies of Type Three.

A healthy Nine who moves to the high side of Three begins to see themselves as successful and significant rather than ineffective and unimportant. They accomplish tasks and increase their confidence.

At the low side of Three, an unhealthy Nine starts to engage in busy work as another way to distract—or narcotize—themselves. They can become workaholics who are really only interested in filling time.

Under stress, Nines shift to Type Six's strategies.

At the high, healthy end of Six, Nines take a stand and become more loyal to themselves and others. They become courageous and willing to take risks for the greater good.

At the low end of Six, however, Nines who haven't achieved their goals become rigid, obstinate, and immobile. Normally trusting, they become paranoid.

Why We All Need the Nines

Of all the things the world has needed—and still needs—peace is high on that list.

And Nines are so important to that process. From Queen Elizabeth II, Dwight D. Eisenhower, and Gerald Ford to Jim Henson, Walt Disney, and Jeff Daniels, Nines down through history have sought to smooth over the rougher parts of life and create things for everyone to enjoy.

Type Nines often serve as mediators for even the most intense conflicts. They want everyone to get along, and much of their energy is spent putting out those fires—both externally and internally.

Nines also have the unique ability to tap into the strengths of the other eight Types. They can be wildly creative, great leaders, enthusiastic helpers, and passionate idealists. They are adept at filling the role that needs filling in intense situations.

Think of John F. Kennedy (a Nine) during the Bay of Pigs situation in the 1960s, where his willingness to make peace most likely saved the world from nuclear armageddon.

Or Abraham Lincoln, putting aside his own personal—and sometimes morally complex—ideals in order to keep the country unified.

These two examples reveal one simple truth. Without the Nines, our world would be a much less peaceful place.

OVERVIEW
Type Nine: The Peaceful Person

Center of Intelligence AUTONOMY

Primary Strategy CULTIVATING HARMONY

Self Image "I AM CONTENT."

Who's on Your Shoulder THE MEDIATOR

Avoidance CONFLICT

Fighting Words "YOU ARE A SELFISH BULLY."

Defense Mechanism NARCOTIZATION

Manipulation TUNING OUT EXPECTATIONS

Speaking Style DE-ESCALATION

Wings TYPES 8 & 1

Complementary Strategies TYPES 3 & 6

CLOSING THE LOOP
(And Opening Your Potential)

One of the main reasons I've written this book is to describe the nine Enneagram Types and show that we are not, as individuals, just one Type. As a complicated animal, you instinctively draw strategies from several Types. You are more than a number.

Figuring out your "main" number and then diving into what that means is fun. And fine.

But that's merely scratching the surface. You only have to watch the evening news to understand how divided our world truly is. We exist in a constant cycle of violent action, reaction, and spin. We are a society of "us vs. them." (Or, at least, that's the story the media has been feeding us for decades.)

The truth remains: Many of us have chosen our clans and can't see beyond the walls we've built.

When those clans clash—often out of fear, and almost always as a result of the blind spots we have for both ourselves and others—that's when real tragedy happens within our society.

So, there's a need—especially now—for people to go deep, to dig in and do the work of figuring out WHY they do what they do.

The only way to accomplish that is to start with the understanding that you, and everyone in your community, draw strategies from points all across the Enneagram.

Wherever you live, you exist within multiple overlapping ecosystems.

Each one of those is Yellowstone all over again.

These ecosystems need all nine strategies to flourish. You need the Powerful, the Wise, the Helping, the Effective, the Loyal—along with all the others—just like the western wilds need the wolves, the elk, the beavers, the bears... all the way down to the crickets and grubs under the rocks.

Every system needs its checks and balances. **Every system requires each of its constituent parts to do what they are designed to do.**

Our systems, if they're going to continue to exist and improve, need the members to learn to get along.

Our ecosystem is emotional, and every one of these nine roles is at play.

The difference between a good ecosystem and a failed one is as simple as this: You have to have people who are living into themselves, increasing empathy, and understanding the strategies that others are using each day.

Now, don't get me wrong. Having a natural, default strategy doesn't excuse immoral behavior. For example, just because a person primarily uses Type One's strategies doesn't let them off the hook for being a judgmental grump. Likewise, someone who scores high in Type Eight isn't morally exempt when they treat others like stepping stones on their way toward personal power. But those tendencies should give you a lens on why people do what they do. It should allow you to better understand both others and yourself.

On a personal level, my research and teaching on the Enneagram have shed a lot of light on my own past.

My father died when I was young. And before that, we had a pretty tense relationship. Through the lens of the Enneagram, though, I've now come to understand why he did some of the things he did and what his motivations were at the time. I also see now why I added fuel to that fire in some situations.

That's what the Enneagram provides. It opens up the individual worlds we each hold within ourselves and lets others in, revealing why we think the way we do.

I hope this book has given you an idea of what balance looks like. Everyone has to do things they dislike, but understanding your strengths and weaknesses can help us all fit together inside our emotional ecosystems.

I also hope I've given you insight into what your proper expectations for others should be.

When you recognize that everyone is different, there's beauty in knowing how—and why—it all fits together.

You can also appreciate that when there are gaps, people using the other eight strategies are there, ready and waiting to step in and fill those needs.

Now that you've read this book, think back to a conflict. An argument. Unspoken tension in a relationship. Strife within your community. Unrest at work.

Knowing what you know now, how could that situation have played out differently?

What motivations were at work?

Do you now have a level of empathy—for both the other person as well as yourself—that might have led to a different outcome?

How has your view of your ecosystem changed after diving deep into what makes us all tick?

At the end of every episode of the *GI Joe* cartoon back in the 1980s, they closed with some timeless wisdom. I'm not sure I can improve upon it, so I'll follow suit:

We're all just looking to satisfy three basic needs—control, belonging, and safety—and we use multiple strategies in the process. Now you know that.

And knowing is half the battle.

Hopefully, now you understand all the lenses at play within the world around you. I hope you have a better insight into where we, as a global community, are right now. I also hope you can see that we're all necessary, that each of us has been designed to fill specific needs in the communities that surround us.

My highest hope, though, is that you can now imagine the possibilities for what can happen when we begin to understand both ourselves and others and work together to build better relationships, better communities and, God willing, a world where we're all living fully into our unique purpose.